Follow the Son

A Gap-Year Adventure with God

David & Janet Simmonds

malcolm down
PUBLISHING

First published 2020 by Malcolm Down Publishing Ltd.
www.malcolmdown.co.uk

24 23 22 21 20   7 6 5 4 3 2 1

British Library Cataloguing in Publication Data
A catalogue record for this book is available from the British Library.

ISBN 978-1-912863-39-6

Cover design by Esther Kotecha
Art direction by Sarah Grace

Printed in the UK

Contents

Dedication

We are delighted to dedicate this book to our six grandchildren – Aliyah, Madeleine, Jamie, Hannah, Felix and Eliot – who have already embraced our spirit of adventure and have travelled widely!

Review

David and Janet Simmonds are two very ordinary people who travelled round the world to mark their retirement. But they quickly discovered that God had plans to use them on their journeys in quite unexpected ways. A very readable book, and a remarkable account.

Cedric Pierce
Retired railwayman who enjoyed a second career in criminal justice.

Introduction

It all began as an idea about ten years beforehand, when David was daydreaming about exploring more of this wonderful world of ours. The idea grew and started to take shape as he studied maps of possible routes, read books by other intrepid travellers and sought advice from experts and organisations. David shared his dream with Janet, and she liked the idea.

We had a friend, a single lady, who had travelled around the world on her own. She inspired us with her courage and exciting tales. We became enthusiastic about all the possibilities and opportunities, but we knew we would have to wait until we retired to have the time and money such a trip would require.

We love to travel. We get excited by new sights and sounds, the jarring and the unfamiliar. We actively seek out oddities. Strange and unusual events are attractive to us. We find novel and weird food appealing – we like to savour the flavour. We forgo the normal in favour of the unknown. We love to take risks and embrace the adventure of the extraordinary. We prefer to go on a local bus rather than jump in a taxi. Where possible, we reject the temptation to compare what we are being presented with, to what we are used to.

Even with our considerable resilience, our adaptability and flexibility were tested to the limit during our year-long adventure. It was a round-the-world trip of a lifetime.

We were conscious of all that we would have to leave behind – our family and friends, our home and garden, our church and, not least, our cat. Of course, we could make practical arrangements, but we knew there would be losses that we would have to face and potential difficulties on our return.

Eventually, the dream won and we were determined to make it happen.

It is important not only to hold onto a dream, but to live in expectation until its fulfilment. Habakkuk 2:3 reminds us 'for the vision is yet for an appointed time . . . Though it tarries, wait for it'.[1] To be grounded in the reality of the vision is as important as being delighted in its hope. We knew we would have to do a lot of planning, but equally we were resolute in keeping the details of the trip to a minimum.

Then came the time when we needed to check it out with our family, our good friends and our church leaders. We knew that we weren't going to be tourists but travellers, not holidaymakers but explorers. It is central in our Christian lives to submit our major decisions to those we trust, in order to receive their advice and insight. Most importantly, we prayed and asked God whether this was His will and purpose for our lives. Everyone, including God, said, 'Yes! Go for it!'

Healing Highlights

Here is a taste of just a few of the healings that God performed as we went round the world:

USA	–	left shoulder
Tahiti	–	emotional hurts
New Zealand	–	57-year-old ladies with hip problems
Australia	–	stroke
Philippines	–	throat tumour
Indonesia	–	breast cancer
Singapore	–	back pain
Malaysia	–	anger, sleep problems and eczema
Thailand	–	head pain, heart problems and fear
Vietnam	–	back problems
Israel	–	bowel cancer

1. New King James Version®. Copyright © 1982 by Thomas Nelson. Used by permission. All rights reserved.

As a couple now married over 40 years, God has blessed us with four sons – Paul, Mark, Chris and John – together with Rachel, whom we will meet again in heaven. We now have three precious daughters-in-law. Sara is married to Paul, and they have two sons, Felix and most recently Eliot, all living in Boise, Idaho. Janelle is married to Mark, and their two daughters, Aliyah and Madeleine living in Plymouth, Michigan. Emma is married to Chris, and their son, Jamie and daughter, Hannah living in Bristol, UK. John lives near London, UK. We met and married in Streatham Baptist Church, 'Lewin', that we attended in South London. Then after we had raised our family, and approached retirement, David heard the audible voice of God telling us 'to go to the coast, but NOT to coast when we got there!' Jesus later confirmed this to us both. We knew it was right to put God first, so we eventually found a wonderful spiritual home with the Beacon Church, Havant. Almost immediately, the Lord directed us to a lovely new (downsized) home, and very quickly after that David got a new job at the University of Chichester, for which he was not really qualified! So, in 2010, we moved to Cowplain, near Portsmouth, on the south coast of the UK. We had given up a great deal to obey this call – our home, our church, our friends, family, jobs, neighbours – only to find that since then God has given us double what we left behind.

What next?

We came to the end of the formal working lives in the summer of 2015. David's employment has always centred around teaching and training adults, helping them to develop their skills, knowledge and confidence in order to fulfil their potential in life. He has trained in Human Resources in industry and commerce, and more latterly serving in the university setting in training trainers – amongst other things. He has written a number of books in the area of training, which have been well received. More recently, he has been exploring the neuroscience of learning. David is a skilled photographer – see the photos in this book; he loves to research family history – our own and other people's; he plays bridge; he loves writing and reading, and real ale!

Janet worked in the NHS first as a nurse, then as a midwife, and finally as a health visitor, which she found to be both challenging and fulfilling, particularly working in the community, supporting young families and building relationships with them. Janet went on to train as a counsellor, and worked first as a volunteer with a Christian counselling agency based at Manna Christian Centre in Streatham. Later she set up her own private practice for over 20 years. She found this fulfilling as she was privileged to see many people come out of prisons of depression, dysfunctional relationships, stress, and loss. Janet's interests include gardening, colour and design, cross stitch to relax, reading, supporting people in different ways, and serving in the local church and community.

Together, they lead South East Hants Healing Rooms in Havant, and as you will see, this aspect of their lives played a key role in their travels around the world.

Travel to discover new places and see more of the world has always been an important facet of their lives. Trips included countries all over Europe, the USA, Croatia, Turkey, Greece, and Israel. David has also done training in six continents – Europe, Asia, Australasia, North America, South America and Africa.

Naturally enough, David had been incubating the idea of travelling around the world for a whole year at some point, for about 10 years, and as retirement came closer, Janet also 'caught the bug'! They started to pray and were encouraged by the positive responses of leaders and friends – not in order to get rid of them for a year! Chris and his wife Emma had spent about 4 months going around the world, going on and off planes quite cheaply, so that seemed to be the best way to travel. Planning included timing – trying to avoid hurricanes and monsoons as much as possible. Leaving the home empty for a year was not an option, and so finally the house was let, creating some additional income, though all our personal possessions had to be packed to go in to storage in the few days before departure.

Farewells

We will never forget our joint retirement weekend, when we were able to celebrate with our family, work colleagues and friends, old and new. It was a wonderful time of laughter, anticipation and thankfulness. However, we hadn't expected the Scripture and prophetic word that was given to us:

> *As you go, proclaim this message: 'The kingdom of heaven has come near.' Heal the sick, raise the dead, cleanse those who have leprosy, drive out demons. Freely you have received; freely give.*

Matthew 10:7-8

'I believe that the Lord is saying to you both:

'"I am setting before you a long, wide, straight road. Walk in it. Do not be afraid, for I will be with you wherever you go. Do not stray to the right or the left but walk along the road that I am giving you. Then you will leave showers of blessing everywhere you go."'

You can imagine how daunted – and yet comforted – we felt. These words were confirmed so many times on our journey. Throughout the year, others prayed that we would have divine encounters and that we would experience things we never had before. On many occasions on our travels, people welcomed us with the delightful greeting that, like Esther, we had come for 'such a time as this' (Esther 4:14).

As we prayed about our journey, we identified three areas on which to focus:

1. Spending time with family and friends in the USA and Australia

2. Visiting many of the natural World Heritage sites in the countries we visited

3. As part of Healing Rooms International, we would visit as many Healing Rooms as we could in the countries where they operate

Healing Rooms International is a Christian ministry of healing. It originated in Spokane and is led by Cal and Michelle Pierce. In just over twenty years, it has spread to about seventy countries. We are directors of South East Hampshire Healing Rooms in Havant, Hampshire, UK. This objective changed the dynamics of our trip beyond anything we could have imagined. It had an impact in terms of the people we met, the places we visited, and our opportunities for ministry. It became the most exciting, challenging and fulfilling aspect of our trip. For more information on Healing Rooms International, see their website.[2]

---

2. www.healingrooms.com

Declarations

As we began our journey, we felt led by God to pray for each nation we visited. As we prayed, God gave us insight into the things He honours in each nation, as well as issues which are preventing them from fulfilling God's destiny. We read a declaration for each country for every day we were in that nation and we believe that as a result, God is bringing about change in those places.

CHAPTER ONE

Beginnings

March – April

David enjoys all the practical arrangements for a holiday – maps, tickets, car hire, and hotels. This time, however, we were faced with the prospect of going to so many countries for such a long time, it proved quite a challenge. We needed to arrange visas and vaccinations; we had to work out how we would cope with all four seasons in two different hemispheres and try to avoid the monsoons. Eventually, we were as prepared as we could be, and agreed to start our adventure on a day that was memorable; St David's Day, the first day of March. Later, we discovered that this was significant because everywhere we went, people would ask, 'Where are you from? When did you start your journey?'

Janet's passion for the expedition was growing and it was becoming infectious. Friends and family wanted to know all about our plans and it soon became clear that they wanted to keep in touch and keep up-to-date with our journey. They had many questions, including, 'How will you manage with just one suitcase and one carry-on bag for a whole year?' As it turned out, it was more difficult than we thought to keep track of the different weight limits for baggage on the various airlines. We had to send stuff home at several points along the way. With only one major exception towards the end of our trip, we never lost our luggage.

Communications

We knew communicating with people was vital and we set up a website and blogsite. However, being able to keep these up to date during our twelve months away was often a major difficulty – things we take for granted at home, in terms of electronic communication, were not always available to us and this became very frustrating.

We were assured, 'All you need is reliable, free access to the internet and a good smartphone with sufficient charge.' However, on more than one occasion, we found that the phone would take over a day to fully charge and the strongest signal was miles away – on one occasion, down by the outdoor food market next to the port.

This caused problems when we needed to book the next flight, hotel or car hire. It was an enduring issue and printing boarding passes was, at times, an insufferable challenge.

With hindsight, we should have done more before we left to encourage people to communicate with us on a regular basis. There were times when both of us, Janet in particular, felt a long way from home. During these times, we would really have liked our friends and family to get in touch with us, just to chat about the everyday, ordinary things in their lives. This was a lesson to us, and now we are trying to improve how we communicate with our friends abroad.

'The Big Apple'

After so much planning and preparation, longing and excitement, we finally left Gatwick Airport on 1 March. As we expected, we had mixed emotions, knowing that we would not be returning home for a whole year. However, New York was beckoning.

We decided to stay in the middle of the (in)famous Manhattan – with all its well-known landmarks – and take advantage of its centrality. One of the things we enjoy is being able to wander around a new place and, where possible, use public transport. We strolled around Central Park in the snow and the landscaped gardens, even in the late winter, were wonderful. Then, we ambled round the Met (the Metropolitan Museum of Art). The exhibits were amazing, in particular the collection of Tiffany stained-glass panels, that catch the light and shimmer with iridescence. Their glowing colours were as fresh as when they were first created.

The cathedral-like stature of Union Station was equally impressive.

We later took the circular tourist bus to get an idea of the whole city and its major sights, including Ground Zero, looking very different now with its landscaped Garden of Remembrance – a memorial to so much loss and devastation, and a place for reflection on the suffering of so many because of the hatred and desire to destroy by a few.

On Friday evening, we had a joyful time at City Light Church where there was great worship, and Pastor Bojan preached on 'grace' from Galatians chapter one. The Holy Spirit was clearly present, and later we ministered to a number of people there.

This was our first visit to 'The Big Apple', and whilst cities are not necessarily our first love, we wanted to explore this iconic place. After a couple of days at our hotel, we decided to speak to the concierge:

'We've only ever seen New York on TV and films. Is it really as bad as that?'

'No!' he exclaimed. *'You'll be fine – Central Park, Madison Avenue, Time Square . . . they're all fine.'*

'Is there anywhere we shouldn't go?'

'Well,' he said hesitantly, *'you should avoid the subway and don't go anywhere near the Bronx.'*

We thanked him for his advice and decided to pray. We really couldn't begin our twelve-month trip in a state of fear and anxiety.

The next day we visited our first Healing Rooms, which meant we had to take the subway, and go to the Bronx! Our time there was remarkable. Right from the very start of our trip, we found true friendship, a warm welcome and tremendous food – and this experience was to be repeated for the remainder of our year. The team of fifteen people asked us to pray for them before they ministered. This too became a model for us over the next twelve months.

Some people requested times of individual prayer and prophecy, while the rest of the team were meeting the visitors. We were really looking forward to seeing what God was going to do and were eager to meet with the team.

Towards the end of our time with each of them, David greeted one of the directors and, as normal, he asked,

'What would you like Jesus to do for you today?'

Before she could reply, David reached out his hand and placed it gently on her shoulder.

'How did you know?' she asked.

'What?'

'I've got a rotator cuff problem, and as soon as you touched it, I could feel God healing me!'

We rejoiced with her and were thrilled that the Lord had come with His healing power in the first week of our trip.

Expectation, faith and hope are closely linked, and God placed a confidence within us that first Saturday that He was going to use us in an extraordinary way throughout the year.

This faith was reinforced as we enjoyed a boat trip round the harbour to view the Statue of Liberty. It was very cold, and we needed to be well wrapped up with the wind whipping around us. We felt God speak very clearly to us:

'We know that where the spirit of the Lord is, there is liberty. So many people are bound by chains of their own making and locked in prisons where the key to the door is in their own hands. Jesus has come to set us free and He has paid the price for our freedom in full.'

After that, we set off – to see the Liberty Bell, in Philadelphia!

Trains, Boats, and Planes

During our adventure, we used a huge range of different modes of transport:

- 5 rental cars and many others belonging to our hosts
- 1 coach from Singapore to Kuala Lumpur
- 1 train – Amtrak from Chicago to Spokane
- 2 boats – a ferry from North to South Island in New Zealand, and from Singapore to Indonesia
- Jeepneys – too many to count, in the Philippines
- Motorised tricycles – too many to count!
- 1 cart – pulled by water buffalo, near Manila
- 1 motorbike – with Janet as the pillion rider, in Vietnam
- Minibuses in Thailand and Vietnam
- There was even a helicopter in New Zealand

The short train ride from Penn Station, New York to 30th Street Station in Philadelphia allowed us to catch a glimpse of the landscape of New Jersey, before meeting Don and Judy – precious family members who had travelled from Harrisburg, Pennsylvania to meet us for a couple of days.

We laughed and cried together as we caught up with all the family news, toured the sights (including the Liberty Bell) and sampled some good beers in The City Tavern – an old colonial property where the staff wear authentic nineteenth-century costumes.

On Wednesday 9 March, we went with Judy and Don to see the grave of David's brother, Colin, for the first time in thirty-two years. Judy had been his wife. The setting was beautiful, and the new headstone was excellent. It was sobering, but healing at the same time. The quietness of the cemetery allowed us all to reflect on Colin's life, and what he had meant to each of us.

Little did we know that we were about to begin (and much later, end) our trip by meeting some lovely Messianic Jewish Christians. We visited their Healing Rooms in Bristol, Pennsylvania and had the privilege of praying with the team and hearing about their ministry. We were impressed by their rich heritage and their passion for Jesus and those who came to them for prayer. We loved all their flags, the music, and Jewish artefacts decorating the rooms.

Next, we flew to Saginaw, Michigan and visited the Healing Rooms at Saginaw Valley Community Church. The large team there had developed a profound and sensitive ministry, which they had recently taken on a mission trip to Nicaragua. This church plays worship music 24/7, sometimes live, sometimes recorded. As we entered the building, we were so aware of the presence of God, and when we arrived at the suite of rooms used by Healing Rooms, we felt God's presence very strongly in the room where visitors wait. Apparently, some visitors are healed there before they even receive prayer from the team! We particularly liked their use of red flags to symbolise the cleansing, healing power of the blood of Jesus.

Meeting with Al and Sheryl, our daughter-in-law Janelle's parents, who live in Flint, was special. We spent some time sharing with them over lunch, and catching up on family news.

One of the benefits of our round-the-world air ticket was that we could fly into New York and later fly out of Los Angeles, and it only counted as one stop. So, to get from the east of the USA to the west, we had two choices:

1. An epic three-week road trip

   or

2. Fly there in just a few hours

In the end, we felt that something in between these two extremes would suit us well. Amtrak provided us with a delightful three-day, two-night journey from Chicago, Illinois to Spokane, Washington. We ate our way through the menu, experienced the unusual pull-out beds, and gasped at the stunning scenery. Our various table companions at dinner were all interested in our gap-year exploits.

Ice and Fire

Our train deposited us in Spokane at 1 a.m. and after a rather bewildering few hours waiting in an empty airport, we flew on to meet Paul, Sara and Felix in Boise, Idaho. We hadn't seen our eldest son and his gorgeous family for nearly fifteen months, so it was great to be able to spend nearly six weeks with them.

While we were staying with them, our pace slowed down considerably, and we were able to settle back into family life. Paul and Sara are both scientists; Paul is a professor of physics and Sara is doing postdoctoral research in biology. Felix is certainly a livewire!

Boise is an appealing city, which showed us all of its charms in the height of spring, with outstanding displays of blossom and early spring flowers. Our family took us up to the foothills of the Rocky Mountains in McCall, Idaho. It was fabulous weather, with sunshine and deep snow. The scenery around Payette Lake was astonishing. The snow, and mountains, and spring flowers were delightful.

But no sooner had we left the snow behind than we were plunged into some hot springs, and then we enjoyed the rest of the drive back to Boise alongside the river in the valley floor.

Resurrection

On the morning of Good Friday, at about the time Jesus would have been crucified, we undertook the strenuous climb of 1,000 feet up Table Rock, near Boise, until we reached the cross at the top. For Janet, it became a pilgrimage. With every step towards the cross, the Lord reminded her of His suffering.

At the top, it was very windy. David asked the Lord what He was saying, and He said, *'Turn to face the wind of My Spirit.'* At that moment, the wind died down and it became extremely still. God reminded us that a plane takes off by flying into the wind. God wants us to fly in the power of His Spirit. Jesus wants us to gaze upon Him, to look full in His wonderful face. As we seek His face and search for the wind of His Holy Spirit, then we will know Him more fully, hear Him more clearly, and feel Him more closely. And at that point, He can guide our every step.

March 25th was also the date that we celebrate our daughter Rachel's birth over 35 years ago, and her brief stay with us before God took her home after just 19 days with us here on earth. Our sadness is always accompanied by our joy in knowing she is now dancing with Jesus in heaven.

Testimonies: Monday 28 March

A few years ago, when David was the chair of trustees at Manna Christian Centre in Streatham, London, yet another demand for an exorbitant rise in rent caused a number of people to urge us to close the ministry. David believed that we should hold onto the original vision; he believed that God had set before us an open door that no man could shut. That Easter Monday, David received a resurrection promise in the form of an email from Howard, the new chairman:

Dear David,

There is so much to say. Here is just a taster from 'Manna House':

We run Friday evenings for the homeless, poor, vulnerable, isolated, and lonely. Over the last year, we have had over fifty people on our books. We share a meal together with plenty of tea/coffee and snacks. We celebrate birthdays with cards and cakes. All are loved and valued.

While some volunteers are sharing with the homeless, etc., others are in the prayer room, and others are on the high street, talking and praying while wearing their 'Manna House' fleeces.

One Saturday morning, Dave Lock, the manager, phoned me to ask why there was a crutch in his office: 'Oh, it must have been left by the homeless lady (rare) who was healed last night.'

We also a had a homeless Polish gentleman with severe back pain who was healed.

A 24-year-old Polish scaffolder was prayed for in the street – he had a broken leg after falling off scaffolding nine months beforehand. He had been back to the hospital to have it rebroken. He couldn't put weight on it and was suffering from arthritis. He was healed. He came back to 'Manna House' and said that he knew we wouldn't understand, as there was no logical explanation for it. This made us all smile.

On the second and fourth Sundays of each month, from 2 p.m. until 4 p.m., we have meals together and share a fresh expression of church – the Holy Spirit is powerfully at work during these times. We are getting all types of people, including the homeless, who come to a church 'for people who don't do church'.

One Sunday recently, we had a lady in her sixties who was sitting down, arms folded and with quite a sour face. Halfway through our time together, one of our homeless Polish gentlemen broke down in tears, and she changed completely – the Spirit was at work. At the end, she came up to me and said, 'Howard, I have been attending a United Reformed Church all my life. My parents told me to always go to church and lead a good life. I have done that religiously, but today I met Jesus for the first time. Thank you.'

Wow! What an honour, privilege and humbling experience this has been, seeing Jesus in the poor and needy. This is just the start of what the Lord has for us. Exciting times. We rely on God and He is faithful and has supplied all we need, whenever appropriate.

Thank you for your continued interest and prayer for the work. God bless you in all your ministries throughout the world. Love & Blessings,

Howard

This was such an encouragement to hear that David's vision had come from the Lord at a time when many felt it was time to quit. Manna Christian Centre continues to serve the community 40 years since it began. God is faithful!

Friday 1 April

We travelled back to Spokane for a training course and conference. It was a privilege to meet Cal and Michelle Pierce and members of their team at the headquarters of the International Association of Healing Rooms. We were blessed to join them in praying for a number of visitors and we witnessed several miracles.

Later, we had a few days on our own in Twin Falls. This is an area riven with a dramatic landscape of deep gorges and rushing rivers, particularly after the snow melt increases the volume of water. Sometime afterwards, we visited a few Healing Rooms in Idaho. After leaving Boise, we received the following note from the director of the Meridian Healing Rooms there:

I think the biggest praise report came from the divine appointment on the phone with Tom. He said his head continued to give him excruciating pain, but he was encouraged to believe and was prompted to go back to his doctor. When they tested him, they found that the device they had put in him to control the pressure on the brain had been set incorrectly and when they reset it, the headaches went away immediately. Praise God. We continue to claim his total recovery. He was praising God.

Our daughter-in-law Sara also sent us an interesting article from *National Geographic*, which explored ways in which long-term travel can change your life. Here are four lessons we learnt from our travels:

Lesson 1: Embrace the Unexpected Detour

This trip thrust us way out of our comfort zone. Our normal practice requires David to over-plan, leading to the inevitable irritations and frustrations that such management and organisation produces. Instead, our adventure forced us to expect the unexpected. For example, in Vietnam, we were asked to be ready for our driver each morning at 8 a.m. We – and often the driver – had no idea where we would be going or what we would be doing.

Lesson 2: Seek Out and Celebrate Diversity

Very early into our expedition, we stopped ourselves from constant comparisons with 'the way we do things back home'. Our Creator God provided us with a rich array of people, food, and situations that were nothing like we had ever experienced. For instance, in the Philippines and Indonesia we tasted a range of extraordinary fruits that we had never even heard of before.

Lesson 3: Live Every Day with an Open Heart

Despite the many language, cultural, and ethnic differences we encountered every day, we found all people everywhere to be essentially the same. Apart from their basic needs of housing, clothing and education, we found that everyone had the same priorities – they cared for their family and friends, they wanted to work, and above all were desperate to be in good health. It was a joy and privilege to stay in the homes of strangers, to share their food, and to be taken to places off the tourist trail.

Lesson 4: Great Risks Lead to Great Rewards

The cliché became true – instead of us affecting people and communities, we ourselves were dramatically changed forever. The greatest lessons that we were taking into our retirement were to live each day as it comes and to ask the Lord, 'Where shall we go? Who shall we meet? What shall we say?'

Declaration for America
March

I love you America; My feisty people born out of a spirit of adventure and a desire for freedom. A land of many people groups and cultures. A nation who has fought for independence, which is a good quality, but has been birthed from a rebellious heart. You work so hard, which I honour, yet the demands you make on yourselves are often at the cost of the relationships that resource you, and also time spent with Me.

At the heart of the nation, in its very beginnings, is the demonic influence of Freemasonry. Many of the founding fathers, and leaders since then, were active Freemasons, evidenced in the design of the Pentagon and symbols on the $1 bill. This Freemasonry is like a yoke that milkmaids carried, with the twin buckets of idolatry and greed.

America, I call you to bow the knee to Me in repentance. I want to remove this yoke that weighs you down and sets limits on your effectiveness for My Kingdom. I see your potential, and if you will come to Me, I will remove and break this yoke. I have a yoke to give you, which is easy and well-fitting.

There are also many people who state an allegiance to Me, but do not yet know Me. My heart is that they will truly encounter Me and that their lives will be transformed by My Holy Spirit.

Many of you have a desire to serve Me in the nation and across the world. As you yield to Me, you will enter into a new freedom, coupled with dependence on Me. Come to Me with surrendered hearts and humbled souls and you will fulfil your destiny as individuals, and as a nation.

Quotes

After watching the River Boise in full spate, and hearing its thunderous noise, we were reminded of the following words:

He will come like a pent-up flood that the breath of the Lord drives along.

Isaiah 59:19

We enjoy using the online devotional *Bible in One Year*,[3] written by Nicky Gumbel. We thoroughly recommend it to you. The following is an example of what we were reading at that time about God's guidance:

There are five main ways in which God guides us (the five Cs):

1. Commanding Scripture (the Bible)

2. Compelling Spirit (the Holy Spirit)

3. Counsel of the Saints (the Church)

4. Common Sense (reason)

5. Circumstantial Signs (providence)

Then on Wednesday 27 April, we also read this: *'The decision to come out of hiding is our initiation rite into the healing ministry of Jesus Christ'* (Brennan Manning).

On 28 April, we made our tearful farewells to our family in Boise, Idaho and flew to Los Angeles. We spent a couple of days exploring the city – although we had visited it two years before when Paul, Sara and newborn Felix were living there. David enjoyed a Thai massage and we had a meal in a Thai restaurant – a taste of things to come.

---

3. www.bibleinoneyear.org

We were also privileged to meet David and Glynda, who have responsibility for Healing Rooms in several states on the west coast. We were blessed by their encouragement and affirmation, as we were about to leave for countries we had never visited before and where we had no contacts.

On our previous visit, Janet had been challenged by God about the angels of Los Angeles (every city has angels) and the fact that they needed to be reawakened. This was especially relevant as there was a revival at Azusa Street in Los Angeles 100 years before, and while we were in America on this occasion, this was being celebrated with a massive gathering of about 80,000 people and a further outpouring of the Holy Spirit was taking place.

Summary

In our first two months, we had (among other things):

- Travelled over 7,160 miles
- Slept in ten different beds
- Eaten mint chocolates laced with jalapeños in a Basque restaurant
- Attended an open-air rock concert
- Watched the *Miracles from Heaven* film in Chicago
- Witnessed many amazing miracles of physical healing

After eight weeks on the road, it seemed like a good time to reflect on our journey so far. It felt like a very long time since we had landed in New York, with the vestiges of heavy snowfall still heaped around the streets.

Overall, we had an amazing time. We had no major issues, apart from leaving our passports in a hotel safe in Saginaw, Michigan, and having to 'wing it' with the security officers at the airport. We were reunited with our precious documents after we arrived in Idaho.

The Highlights

Spending time with family and friends was so special. We valued seeing Don and Judy in Philadelphia and Al and Sheryl in Michigan. We loved our time with Paul, Sara and Felix in Idaho, together with Sara's parents, Roy and Suzie, who flew in from Minneapolis. We are so blessed and privileged to have such a family and enjoyed precious times with them all.

Felix, who was almost 2 years old at the time, had a preoccupation with all things vehicular, and we often went out with him to try and see diggers, cranes, motorbikes, and emergency vehicles of all kinds – all with varying degrees of success.

Special places we visited included:

- The urban waterfalls in Spokane
- The 'Glory Room' at the Healing Rooms HQ in Spokane, where the presence of God was tangible
- The mountains of Montana coated in snow
- Table Rock in Boise, on Good Friday

We also had a wonderful time with leaders and teams of eight different groups of people who minister at Healing Rooms across the USA. We felt sad saying goodbye to them, even after spending only a couple of hours sharing and praying with them, knowing we may not see them again this side of heaven. They enriched us and we learned a great deal from them. We found that we were equipped to be able to encourage groups of people with all that we had learned.

CHAPTER TWO

New Horizons

May – June

Sometimes you are able to have a stopover at a connecting airport when you are en route to your final destination. On our way to New Zealand, we had a stopover, for two weeks in Tahiti!! And in terms of our round-the-world ticket, it still didn't count as a stop.

On arrival at the airport, we were greeted by a trio singing a traditional welcome using local instruments and wearing traditional costumes. This was a taste of things to come later in the Far East.

Our first impressions were of the beauty of the island. Most of the women wear a flower in their hair, and there are plenty of garlands and flower decorations available to buy as part of the tourist industry of the island. It is very verdant and fertile; dense jungle and steep hills produce amazing flowers everywhere.

We quickly became aware of the contrast in lifestyle between the wealthy tourists – who provide the main income for Tahiti – and the local people, 60 per cent of whom are unemployed. Tahiti was once a French colony, but unusually, the people had embraced the Protestant faith. We learned that the Tahitians have multi-ethnic origins from France, the Philippines, and other Polynesian nations. We later discovered that their national language is similar to the Māori tongue, as settlers from the Philippines and Indonesia had travelled in log canoes by sea to New Zealand over 1,000 years ago, and from there to Polynesia.

The weather in Tahiti is always hot and humid. This was our first encounter with such a climate on the trip, and we found that after a couple of hours outside, we had to retreat to a place where there was air conditioning. Inevitably, this meant that the pace of life is generally a lot slower. However, things in Papeete the capital are rather more hectic.

Our hotel overlooked the harbour and we could watch vessels large and small entering and leaving this haven in the South Pacific. One evening we ate at a high-end French restaurant, which was similar to European prices, so after that we enjoyed tasty and much cheaper fare down at the 'hawker stands'. These were mobile units that appeared from 5.30 p.m. to 10 p.m. each evening and served a wide variety of different cuisines – Chinese, Italian, fast food, seafood . . . the smells, sights and sounds overwhelmed our senses. Dining was al fresco on picnic tables, sitting with total strangers. It was also fascinating to watch the rats scurrying round for titbits.

Curiously, there was an excellent public Wi-Fi signal available nearby, so we took advantage of the internet there. We also regularly sat in a local open-air restaurant over a coffee that lasted an hour or two, just to be able to use their internet signal. These locations became an invaluable resource, since the 'free WiFi' advertised in the hotel existed only in about 3 square metres of the lobby, and we had to pay for the vouchers.

As we prayed for these island people, the Lord gave us the following words, which we continued to declare over Tahiti in the ensuing months:

Declaration for Tahiti
May

My people of Tahiti, formed from your indigenous groups and from other nations who have come to your shores over the centuries. I love you. I love your vibrancy, your enthusiasm, your colourfulness, your tenacity, your creativity, your national flower that symbolises your fragrance to Me. I love the way you have embraced Me, My teachings, My truth.

Your patriotic song 'Long Live Tahiti Nui' declares:

God created my country
Garland of multiple islands
With such delicate fragrances
Linked up as an everlasting braid
Today let me praise You
Listen to Your children's voice
Crying out 'Lavish Your Love'
So that Tahiti Nui can live.

Your rich, varied heritage is a blessing, but you are uncertain about who you are as a nation and as individuals. I want you to discover something new about your value and worth. As children accept and receive parents' unconditional love based on who they are, not what they achieve, I want you to know and experience My unconditional love for you. I loved you before you knew Me.

I want to do a new thing on your islands. I call you to come together in unity; to stand together, to pray together, to worship together. Forget the things that separate you and instead celebrate all you have in common. I have poured out My Spirit on these islands before, but My heart is to do a new thing; a work of My Spirit which will transform communities. To bless you and to make your streets safe places. To see My love bringing hope and freedom and a future.

We had been given only one contact address in the nation – for David and Erin Burr, who were Youth with a Mission (YWAM) team leaders on the island. We were able to meet with them on several occasions. Sometime later, after we had left the island, we were so encouraged to receive this follow-up message:

> *It was lovely meeting you both and we are so thankful for the time we got to spend with you. Thank you again for treating us to lunch and for coming to our teaching nights. It was a blessing to have you here in Tahiti! Thank you so much for sending over the declaration for Tahiti – I'm excited to read over it and begin to declare it as well ☺ Your word of 'fighting and possessing our inheritance' has been on our hearts as well. It isn't like God speaks something, you arrive at your destination and then it just happens automatically – there is fighting to possess and hold what God has given. Thank you for your prayers on this front. We want to be strong and courageous and continue to fight for all God has for French Polynesia.*
>
> *Blessings to you both as you continue to travel ☺ We will continue to think of and pray for you two. Praying we may meet with you again someday, here in Tahiti or somewhere else.*
>
> *David & Erin Burr, YWAM Leaders*

Through David and Erin, we were introduced to a local church which worshipped in the back streets of Papeete. The building was a house that opened out towards the rear on Sundays, so we were mostly out in the open. It was a small congregation of around forty to fifty people, who spoke a mixture of their native tongue and French.

At the end of the service, David shared some words of knowledge the Lord had given him earlier and together we prayed for most of the congregation. Unfortunately, in the background, enthusiastic music was played by the worship band. Because of our limited knowledge of French and the lack of an interpreter, this made praying for people quite a challenge.

There was one special word David shared:

'There is a little girl here who was upset by a friend in the school playground last week and you hid behind a tree crying. Jesus wants you to know that He saw this and was with you when that happened.'

To David's surprise, no one responded. The other words of knowledge had all seemed so accurate and people had responded and been prayed for, However, after the service, a mother brought her young daughter forward saying that she had not heard what David had said because she had been in Sunday school. She was visibly blessed that Jesus had seen her distress and bothered to tell a stranger about it. God cares about the details of the lives of all His children.

We also met the pastor, John, a gentle and humble man who has significant access to and contact with the government. He told us how, on one occasion, he was meeting the Minister of Finance and while he was still talking to this man, God took John in the Spirit to the Pentagon in the USA.

God said to him, *'What would you like for your people?'*
'To provide financial help for them,' John replied.

At the end of his meeting, he met a Christian friend who worked for the government and he told her of his spiritual experience. Her response was significant: 'I can't tell you the details, but what you have told me is relevant to what is happening now.' Pastor John later heard that at that very time the Pentagon had been discussing offering a huge sum by way of financial aid to the nation and had decided to give a substantial sum of money! God cares about Tahiti!

We also went on a tour of the island in a taxi, visiting various places of interest. There is one main road round the edge of the island from which all of the villages and coastal resorts are accessed. The centre is a mountainous, impenetrable region, although some of the native people still live there.

Our hotel did not have beach facilities, so we visited another hotel for the day and enjoyed their amenities instead. Yes, it looks just as it does in the adverts, with the thatched huts in the sea!

Our time in French Polynesia was a wonderful experience of God's blessing, Jesus' favour and the Holy Spirit's presence. Evidence of His amazing creation was everywhere. We were blessed with times of rest and refreshment. More than anything, we were humbled by the way He used us in ministry with members of the local YWAM team.

We were also asked to pray for a team of local Christians who were just about to embark on a mission trip to New Zealand. They would be landing there only a few days before us. Because of the strong ethnic links with the Māori people, the group wanted to develop relationships with those in New Zealand and strengthen connections between these island people groups. They were going to use native music and dance to make cultural ties with descendants of the original inhabitants of New Zealand. The Māori tongue also has similarities to the native Tahitian language, so they would be able to understand each other. Ironically, we were unable to connect with the group when we arrived in New Zealand as we had no phone contact details for the group!

It is quite mind-blowing the way in which Jesus is moving the people of His family to communicate with others in different countries. We met this team of Tahitians before they went on mission to New Zealand. Later, when we were in New Zealand, we met a number of Māori Christians. Later still, we met a team of Samoans from New Zealand who were on a mission trip to Thailand!

While we were in Tahiti, our own family from the UK and USA were all meeting together for a short holiday in North Wales and we were able to 'join' them via a largely unsuccessful Skype call – technology, eh? It was so special that they could all meet, but as you can imagine, we really wanted to be there too, rather than somewhere in the South Pacific. A good friend of ours, Alison, met up with them all, and Sara took the photo.

A New Continent

Our flight from Tahiti to Auckland caused a slight administrative hiccup; although it was technically one flight from the USA to New Zealand, with a two-week stopover in Tahiti, we were being flown by a different airline who had different rules about baggage allowance. And on the second leg they were much less generous. We endured an embarrassing scene at check-in when we had to open all our suitcases in public view and under the condescending gaze of the staff, shifting loads of items around, until eventually we managed to avoid a costly excess-baggage bill.

We left Papeete Airport on 15 May and arrived at Auckland Airport on 16 May. During the course of the flight, we crossed the International Date Line – which meant we lost twenty-four hours, and will never get it back!

During our first week in Auckland, we were staying in the Shakespeare Hotel, and our room was located at the top of ninety stairs, so we got a good workout several times a day.

We had a great opportunity to explore the city; we enjoyed high-class food at reasonable prices; and visited Waiheke island, just offshore from Auckland, with its beautiful white sand beaches; we visited Auckland Museum; and we learnt more about New Zealand. For example, the Māori name '*Aotearoa*' means 'land of the long white cloud' because that's what the early settlers saw when they first travelled in their canoes across the Pacific Ocean from the Philippines and Indonesia and discovered the land about 800 years ago. We also learned the Māori word '*kiaora*' means 'welcome', which is a little different to the name of the orange juice we enjoyed when we were growing up.

An amazing display of traditional Māori song and dance thrilled us, together with the *haka*, which will be familiar to any rugby fans who have watched the All Blacks play.

In the north of New Zealand, the climate is sub-tropical, and it has active volcanoes and hot springs, particularly in the Rotorua area. The land is reasonably flat, and it does not take long to travel from the east to the west coast. Further south there is a ridge of mountains, which we later traversed safely.

After we rented a car, we were able to explore the whole of the Coromandel Peninsula, which is about 1 and a half hours from Auckland. Most recommended road trips in the area take 3 days – but we did it in one day, which surprised the locals! The journey consisted of over seven hours driving on extremely curvy roads but the landscape was amazing.

We saw where Captain Cook first landed and named the area 'Thames' – perhaps he was feeling homesick. We also noticed that people were not wearing shoes, even though this was their winter. We later discovered that it is a lifestyle choice of many New Zealanders in the North Island area, where they choose to go barefoot, and they are very proud of it.

We left Auckland on 24 May. We travelled up to Warkworth, which in Māori means 'open heaven'. There we met Julie Calvert who was the National Director of over fifty Healing

Rooms in New Zealand at that time. We found her inspiring; she is a visionary, moving in the power of the Spirit. She also has tremendous energy and has received many prophecies about New Zealand being in the vanguard of what God wants to pour out on the nations.

Through Julie, we later met Christians all over New Zealand; we were able to pray with a number of the teams and give teaching to different groups. Some of Julie's friends, Peter and Wendy Bratty, had generously offered to host us in a holiday apartment for a week in Snells Bay. It was incredibly luxurious! We really enjoyed walking along the wide sandy beach outside the apartment and couldn't quite believe the mild weather. It was still difficult to get our heads round the fact that it was winter in May.

Another day in paradise!

While we were in the area, Julie arranged for us to have lunch with some friends – David, Christine and their 8-year-old son, Sam. They run Healing Rooms on the outskirts of Auckland, which we later visited. When visitors come for healing, the couple spend time praying with them, while their son is in another room drawing prophetic pictures for the visitors, which are amazingly accurate. He later did some drawings for us when we went there. We were led to pray God's blessing and abundance for this precious family.

One evening, we were invited to share with a gathering of those involved in prayer ministry. We shared how we had come to be there and spoke of our vision for the coming year. We talked about healing and some of the different ways that God heals. Then, David shared some words of knowledge for healing and several people came forward for prayer.

Faithful to our original objective to experience God's wonderful creation, over the next two days, we explored the area about 50 miles north of Auckland. We visited Omaha Beach, with its dazzling white sand. We went to Matakana Market, a place which is popular with the locals and where you can buy an astonishing selection of locally grown fruit and vegetables. Our visit to a marine research centre on Goat Island was very informative. We learned that sea birds can live for up to forty years as they are less vulnerable there to predators. We also discovered that fish can talk! On 26 May, we were directed by God to attend Gateway Church near Snells Bay, which met in a scout hut. We had a special time of worship and David had the opportunity to share some words of knowledge for healing. The congregation gasped when he said that he believed someone in the church had recently been diagnosed with leukaemia. Just two days earlier, a lady in the church had just received such a diagnosis. Although she was not at the meeting that morning, we had the privilege of praying for her the next day, after she invited us to come to her home.

Later that Sunday, after a bring-and-share lunch at the pastor's home, two of the members were baptised in the sea, in the middle of winter. They were older men who had come to know Jesus after struggling with some major issues in their lives. It was moving to see them standing on the wet and windswept beach, testifying to their new-found faith in Jesus and proclaiming their desire to follow Him for the rest of their lives.

We were also privileged to meet and pray with Julie's husband, Max. Julie told us that New Zealand is one of the newest nations on earth; it was uninhabited 1,000 years ago but has always readily received the gospel.

The Māori people invited missionaries to come and tell them about Jesus in the early 1800s, and they were visited by spiritual giants like Smith Wigglesworth in the twentieth century. We visited one church where Smith Wigglesworth preached. Perhaps as a result of this, they are more open and willing to hear and respond to the voice of God and take His message to the nations.

Visiting the Healing Rooms in Warkworth, praying with the team, and praying with several visitors who had come for healing, proved to be so heartening for us.

We enjoyed some lovely walks along the beach, and several amazing sunsets. Having time to explore the area, we tasted some of the locally produced wine – excellent! The country is very fertile, producing an abundance of fruits: apples, citrus fruit, bananas, grapes, olives, and of course, kiwi fruit.

On 31 May, we were on the road again, heading further north to Whangarei, where we had been invited to stay with John and Helen McGregor. John is director of the Healing Rooms there. He and his wife are inspirational; they are involved in so many local activities that they have won awards for their service to the community. They have real servant hearts.

The day after we arrived, John helped us to tick off one of the items on our 'bucket list' by taking us up to the Bay of the Islands, and on to where a significant document called the 'Treaty of Waitangi' was signed in 1840. This was the beginning of a time of restitution for the Māori people (which to some degree is ongoing) as there was much suffering, loss and injustice at the hands of the British.

Feeling very diffident about going to such a place, we were instead greatly blessed as there has been a lot of restorative intercession there. We felt an overwhelming sense of God's peace in a place that has known an immense amount of bloodshed and hatred. The land has been cleansed. During that time, the team from Tahiti came to pray in the area, although we were disappointed not to meet up with them.

By way of contrast, we visited some quirky toilets in Kawakawa designed by a certain Mr Hundertwasser. These conveniences were commissioned by the town as they didn't have any public toilets; since then they have become such a magnet for tourism that the economy of the town has been revived.

On 2 June, we travelled for over five hours to Whakatane to stay with John and Jeannie Bentley, who are directors of Healing Rooms there. We had some time to explore the area the next day and saw White Island with its active volcano puffing away in the bay. From Jeannie, we learned that the first native canoe to arrive at Whakatane was called 'Matakane' which means 'the face of God' – we thought that was pretty awesome.

The next town was Rotorua. We could smell the city long before we arrived and were fascinated by the sight of steam coming up through the drains. It was swathed in mist.

We had been invited to attend the opening of a new Healing Rooms in the city centre. Just a year before we arrived, an amazing lady called Joy Bennett had been sent by God from a nearby town to live in Rotorua. When she arrived, God told her to start Healing Rooms. At the last minute, and in a room full of about forty people, David was asked to bring a message. He also tentatively shared that he felt there was a lady, aged 57, who had problems in her hip. We were astonished when TWO 57-year-old ladies approached us with hip problems. God cares so much. We were at the launch a lot longer than expected as we prayed for many people. Unfortunately, this meant that we didn't have time to visit the set of Hobbiton. Soon after we arrived, the Lord gave us the following declaration for New Zealand:

Declaration for New Zealand
May

You are a land born from volcanic eruption, peopled by those who travelled to your shores and claimed it as their homeland; some in the past, others more recently. These islands have known upheaval, conflict, bloodshed, and violence over the centuries. As in the natural birthing of this land, so in the spiritual; created from fire. I will make a new creation by the fire of My Spirit. Look and see what I am about to do.

Your Creator calls you to know His reconciliation among your people. The path has been made through Jesus' death and resurrection:

> *. . . and through Him to reconcile to himself all things, whether things on earth or things in heaven, by making peace through His blood, shed on the cross.*

(Colossians 1:20)

You are a welcoming nation. You open your islands to people from across the globe. You are a sanctuary for many. I value your perseverance, commitment, courage, and compassion.

To those who already know Me; I have so much more for you as you lay aside your restricted beliefs and expectations. As you enter into a deeper personal relationship with Me, I want to reveal My presence, show My power, bring unity and understanding to your communities, overthrow those strongholds you have allowed Satan to establish, and establish instead My everlasting Kingdom rule.

Others who have not known Me but seek meaning and purpose in other expressions of spirituality, will turn to Me in these days, as they see My Church rising up, standing together in repentance, reconciliation and prayer, and can see Me at work transforming lives.

Seek Me and I will reveal Myself to you in My love and in My cleansing, healing, and transforming power. I am only a prayer away! I love you. You are a small nation with a big heart. I long for you to experience My Father's embrace.

That evening, we knew how Joseph and Mary felt in Bethlehem as we hadn't made a reservation for a room, and the whole town was booked up. We were told it was something to do with the island celebrating Queen Elizabeth's 90th birthday! We were delighted to see how proud they are of the Queen. Joy Bennett came to the rescue and offered us her spare bedroom.

After this, despite dire warnings from the locals about such a long and treacherous journey, we had an easy, safe and comfortable drive over the mountains to Napier, a seaside town on the east coast. The town has more Art Deco buildings than anywhere else in the southern hemisphere. It had been flattened by an earthquake in the early 1930s, so the town planners decided to rebuild in the style of the time. The delightful architecture reminded us so much of the buildings in the TV series *Poirot*.

From the coast, we wended our way further south until on 6 June we arrived in Wellington. The capital city is situated at the southern tip of North Island. There we met another lovely couple, Chris and Ruth Miles, who are directors of one of the Healing Rooms in the city. A few days before we had arrived, there had been an earthquake, which registered 5.5 on the Richter scale. Chris told us that the chance of another earthquake was high and gave us a briefing on what to do if it happened. There were no earthquakes or tremors while we were there, which Janet found quite disappointing, though the local people were relieved.

Chris and Ruth arranged a meeting at their home for a number of people from different Healing Rooms. We shared and prayed with those who came, and again saw the Lord move in healing power; back pains were healed. David shared his own testimony of how God had healed him of an incurable spinal condition known as spondylolisthesis over forty years previously:

At that time, and after many tests and examinations, David was told by the hospital consultant that he had an incurable back problem, which could only be managed with painkillers for the rest of his life. He was in a lot of pain and was even unable to pick up our 9-month-old first-born son, Paul. So, David prayed and very simply asked God to heal him. But he heard God speak audibly to him, and He told David He wasn't going to heal him! Instead was going to complete the healing He had already paid for at the cross. After prayer at our church in London, David was instantly and miraculously healed. That day, all his pain disappeared, and he has since lifted many heavy loads and pushed cars, proving the long-term effects of God's healing. But he hadn't bargained on the prophetic word that accompanied the healing miracle, God said to him that He was giving him healing, not just for himself, but so that he could give it away to others. God commissioned David to pray for others to be healed. He has tried to remain faithful to that call ever since.

Statistics

At this point in our journey, we had travelled 12,500 miles by air. In just three weeks since arriving in New Zealand we had:

- Driven approximately 1,200 miles
- Visited 7 Healing Rooms and ministry teams
- Shared and prayed for people at churches in:
  - Auckland
  - Warkworth
  - Rotorua
  - Westport
  - And many other home groups and gatherings

Praise God for all He has done.

On Wednesday 9 June, we left North Island by ferry to go across the Cook Strait to Picton. We were delighted to have a smooth, if slightly protracted, journey which lasted four hours and thirty minutes. For the captain to be able to manoeuvre such a vast ship in the narrow inlets between South Island and Arapawa Island had our greatest admiration. When we arrived, we were hosted by Graham and Pam Wadsworth, who live in Blenheim in the Marlborough Valley. Pam is on the local Healing Rooms team. They were intrigued to learn that we had visited Blenheim Palace in the UK, where the Duke of Marlborough has his seat. We also told them of its links to Winston Churchill and Princess Diana.

South Island is known for its vineyards, and further south there are dramatic fjords or 'sounds' where they have some of the highest rainfall in the world. The backbone of the island has a high ridge of mountains called the Southern Alps, which extends most of the length. South Island also has skiing facilities in the winter.

It also boasts Fox Glacier, which sadly with global warming is diminishing in size.

The next day we visited the Marlborough area, where most of the native fruit orchards have now been given over to vineyards. Highfield Winery produces high-quality wine and we enjoyed sampling their wares over lunch. Then, we visited a nearby chocolate factory – tasting delicious wine and chocolate in one day. After an evening with some of the Healing Rooms team, we left for Greymouth on the west coast of South Island. We stayed in a charming motel and were well provided-for. The town did indeed look rather grey as we arrived in the rain, but the weather improved the next day.

One of the major differences between the North and South Islands is the weather. It rains a lot more in the south because of the dominating Southern Alps that form a backbone right down the centre of the island and the clouds tend to drop their huge amounts rain on the west coast.

The next day, a must-see was the Pancake Rocks or Punakaiki – they were amazing. Formed by the power of wind and rain, the rocks have eroded into what look like enormous stacks of pancakes. A lot of time and investment have been put into creating the walkways so that you can see these spectacles – plus the ferocious blowholes, which dramatically erupt with water, especially when the sea is rough.

On our way there, we travelled along the Great Coast Road, which winds up from Greymouth to Westport. This is a sinuous road which consists of a combination of steep inclines and descents. It is among the top ten greatest coastal drives in the world, and we were fortunate enough to drive it twice. There were so many hairpin bends, it would have kept a nineteenth-century hairdresser happy for days. The views were astonishing, and we took turns driving so we could both experience the sights safely.

Coast!

Even on a calm day, the sea there is quite turbulent and is favoured by surfers. The rock formations, of which the Pancake Rocks are only a part, are so dramatic and provide an impressive backdrop to the sea.

Scan the QR codes to watch the videos

We left Greymouth on Sunday 11th and travelled up the Great Coast Road again to visit Steve and Clenda Wockner in Westport. Steve is the vicar of St John's Anglican Church in the town. They had invited us to come to the morning service and share what was on our hearts. Our mutual friend Pam from Blenheim had been in touch with Steve and had suggested he might like to have us to visit.

We had a wonderful time meeting with their congregation and later prayed for some of them. David rose to the occasion to speak and between us we led the service, which was a surprise – we were learning to expect surprises. David had some words of knowledge, including one for a person who was having problems with their ears, but it was not to do with hearing. An elderly lady came to us and said that she had 'balance problems'. We prayed for her and she abandoned her walking frame and walked down the church unaided, and then she ran back up the aisle. Praise God!

We stayed overnight with the Wockners, after enjoying delicious whitebait patties made by Clenda. These are a delicacy on the west coast. They took us on a local tour and we were enchanted to be shown some beautiful, dramatic, windswept places in the area, including Cape Foulwind, which had originally been named by Captain Cook, who had a reputation for naming places he discovered. We don't think he liked it much.

We were impressed with the high value the islanders placed on conservation and protecting the land from infestation from outside. For example, we even had to have our luggage scanned coming in to New Zealand to ensure we weren't importing fruit, vegetables or other products that could be harbouring pests, as this could damage their delicate flora and fauna. We also heard that school children replant shrubs and plants that are native to the land, particularly where there is risk of coastal erosion.

On our journey down the west coast of South Island, we encountered a dramatic, awe-inspiring landscape. Towering mountains filled the horizon and on 14 June, we had the thrill of a helicopter trip up to the top of Fox and Franz Josef Glaciers and Mount Cook. While we were there we wondered if there was a connection with Fox's Glacier Mints!

It was extremely overcast that day and for a while it seemed as if we would be unable to fly, but then there was a window in the clouds and some heavenly sunshine; suddenly, we were airborne. The exhilaration was so great, we almost clapped! Thank you, God! We were able to get out at the top of Mount Cook and walk around in the snow. We were told that Fox Glacier is the third fastest moving glacier in the world, which probably means more to geologists than it did to us. It was a beautiful ice-blue colour in places and the flat vastness of snow and ice looked like the icing on one of Janet's Christmas cakes.

In contrast to this snowy scene, later that day we visited the Franz Josef Glacier hot pools just down the road, where we were surrounded by tropical rainforest. New Zealand is truly a land of astonishing contrasts.

Later, when we visited Haast further down the coast, it was more stark and rugged. Most people who travel there will hike and enjoy the untouched nature of the landscape. There are areas of dense rainforest where the trees have not been cut down. South Island is always green. There are also very few shops in the area of Jackson Bay. We wondered where the local people get their daily bread and milk from.

On 17 June, we drove over the mountains to Queenstown, which is situated on Lake Wakatipu – the longest lake in South Island – formed in a glacial valley. The roads were exciting with many hairpin bends and amazing views. We stopped to see Roaring Billy Falls descending into another glacial valley – awesome! We were relieved that our small car coped with the steep hills and that there was no snow. The weather was unusually mild during our visit and we were told the skiers were frustrated with the lack of snow. Apparently, they use artificial snow machines if there isn't enough.

In Queenstown, we treated ourselves to a hotel overlooking the lake, rather than a motel and we enjoyed the additional facilities.

At 5.30 a.m. on 18 June, we were preparing for our strenuous daytrip to Doubtful Sound – another name imparted by Captain Cook. We travelled by coach to Lake Manapouri, which has one of the biggest hydroelectric power stations in the country and provides 18 per cent of New Zealand's electricity. By now, a steady drizzle had begun and we set out for a boat trip across the lake.

Then a bus took us down Wilmot Pass, which is the only road in the country that is not part of a road network as it only links two lakes. We were told that it was completed in 1965, at taxpayers' expense, to provide a way to transport the materials to build the power station. During the construction, one lorry lost its grip on the road, and ended up hurtling back down the hill damaging the road, resulting in a costly bill.

We were also told that on occasions, the rainfall has been so heavy that part of the road is washed away. We were reassured that if our return was delayed, a helicopter would be dispatched to bring us all back. We had mixed feelings of both relief and disappointment when there was no helicopter waiting to airlift us back on our return.

Travelling down Wilmot Pass was an adventure in itself, because this was the steepest road we had been on ever, anywhere in the world. The 1-in-3 winding narrow roads had no room for oncoming traffic either. The rain continued unrelenting, which was to be expected since the area has an annual rainfall of 25 feet a year, and that it rains 300 days out of 365! It was hardly surprising that we had a wet day, especially as the wettest weather occurs in the winter. Sometimes the rain is so heavy that parts of the cliffs collapse, taking trees and shrubs down into the water. The vegetation is lush, and lichens are abundant.

The cliffs were 1 kilometre high and the wet weather meant that waterfalls cascading down the cliffs were a spectacular sight. Apparently, most of the waterfalls disappear when there is a spell of dry weather. At least we were not bothered by sand flies as it was raining.

We had two more days exploring the area, including Arrowtown, formerly built when 'gold was found in that there river'. Many of the original buildings have been restored and preserved, giving a sense of what life was like there 150 years ago. The Arrowtown museum was one of the best we have ever visited; it had extensive representations of what life would have been like as a farmer, a shoemaker, a gold miner, a wheelwright, a wife, a mother, and a child. It was an interesting place – even the toilet was funny. It was part of the display in the museum and when you opened the door, the enthroned figure of a man holding a newspaper said gruffly, 'Can't you see I'm busy?' Well, Janet thought it was amusing!

On 21 June, we departed for Gore and the weather was starting to clear up. Gore was settled by many miners of Scottish origin. This lives on in the names of many towns, such as Invercargill, and in the road names of the area. Many of the folk in Gore also have a marked roll to their 'R's when they speak. We also noticed that a number of girls' schools on the east coast wear tartan kilts as part of their uniform.

We were hosted by Bill and Karen Kirk who live in Tapanui. Karen is the director of Healing Rooms in Gore, which is the southernmost Healing Rooms in the world. We were privileged to meet with over twenty people there, where we shared our story and prayed for many people who were visiting.

Two days later, we were on the road again to visit Dunedin (another name for Edinburgh, so the Scot's influence continued). Every other road had a Scottish name, and the designs and materials used reminded us of the Scottish capital.

The roads were very steep. We huffed and puffed our way up a long 1-in-3 hill and were glad we didn't have to do it every day. As we couldn't afford the expensive tickets to watch Wales play the All Blacks, we saw the match in the pub.

Taking in some of the local culture, and echoing some memories of National Trust properties in the UK, we were enthralled by Olverston House, a Victorian property, which has been amazingly preserved. The house and all its contents were bequeathed to the nation by the last owner on her death.

Before we left Dunedin, we visited Larnach Castle, complete with turret and flagpole, but no drawbridge. The staircase was amazing winding up through the centre of the house. A real masterpiece! It has a sad past, which includes two family members, father and son, taking their lives when things became too difficult for them. Our last stop on the road north was at Timaru, a few miles south on the coast. We were warmly welcomed at South Life Church.

In Christchurch, we were deeply shocked by the continued scenes of desolation from the earthquakes in 2010 and 2011. There are vast, empty areas where large buildings once stood. One hundred and eighty-five people died and the lives of so many others were changed forever through the devastation of their homes, the loss of their loved ones, and the ongoing effects of tragic injuries. Nevertheless, the city is busy rebuilding. Some parts are a maze of cranes and scaffolding.

It was disturbing to see real-time footage of the earthquake, which had been recorded on a traffic camera. We watched as a street of buildings disintegrated in a few seconds, as if a demolition button had been pressed without any warning. The people there are resilient and determined to get on with their lives; although some opted to leave, most people stayed in the city. Our hotel was on the edge of the quake zone and our room was so tiny we referred to it as a 'pod-pad'!

We visited the Cardboard Cathedral, an innovative structure, which really is made out of cardboard. It was designed by Japanese architect Shigeru Ban, who did not charge for his work. The cathedral is all the more poignant when you realise that a number of those who died in the earthquake were from Japan. In fact, just a few months afterwards, a team of volunteers from Christchurch went to help the Japanese in the wake of the tsunami at Fukushima. The cathedral looked like a huge white tent with beautiful, stained-glass windows. It is supposed to be a temporary structure, but rumour has it that it may well survive long after the old cathedral is repaired or rebuilt.

We met people from several Healing Rooms in the area, and ministered to the teams. We became aware of the stress of living in an area which could have another earthquake at any time, although there is a dogged resistance to moving away from the area because it is, after all, home to them. After our visit to Christchurch, we said goodbye to New Zealand. We thanked God that the only problem we encountered in over six weeks of travelling was a cracked windscreen on our hire car.

Our next stop was Sydney.

CHAPTER THREE

Down Under

July – August

Australia has an important place in the psyche of most British people. It appears to be so far away, so big, and so empty. And yet, many of us know someone who lives there, or someone who emigrated there long ago. Many people have a yearning to visit, but the distances are so vast and other demands on our time and money are so urgent that making any form of meaningful holiday seems daunting.

Several years ago, David was flying to Melbourne and the pilot announced that Perth was visible on the left if you looked below. *Better buckle up and prepare to land,* he thought to himself. After that announcement, it took another four hours for the plane to cross this huge continent.

We arrived in Sydney at the beginning of July and stayed in a hotel in the centre of the city. We had beautiful 'winter' weather as we explored the city on a bus tour, visiting iconic places like Bondi Beach. We marvelled at the views of Sydney Opera House and in the wealthy suburbs there were a surprising number of buildings from the late nineteenth century. Later, we took the ferry across the harbour to Manly, past Sydney Harbour Bridge which is as amazing in real life as it is in the photographs. We decided not to do the walking tour over the top of the bridge.

On Sunday 3 July, we found a Baptist church whose congregation was mostly Chinese and was led by a Chinese pastor. We opted for the English-speaking service.

One of the delights of our year-long trip was the way in which local people wanted to show us around and take us off the beaten track, away from the tourist traps. We met Franklyn and Dianne Elliott, directors of Healing Rooms in Australasia, who took us on an extensive tour of the shoreline around Sydney, which extends some 240 kilometres. Seeing the amazing coastline, and some of their favourite places and beaches, we ended our tour with the perfect meal – fish and chips. It was an opportunity to get to know them, for us all to share stories, and to explore together our joint vision about what God wants to do in the southern hemisphere.

Franklyn and Dianne often visit the Muslim nation of Indonesia to encourage the work of Healing Rooms, even in the prisons. This was helpful in preparing us for our visit there later in the year. Franklyn spoke to us of prisoners who are on death row for drug-trafficking and other offences and told us of the effect on their lives as they meet with Jesus and commit themselves to Him. Despite their death sentence, they are transformed and although they have little hope of reprieve, they live their lives joyfully in the knowledge that they have been forgiven. They can look forward to being in heaven with Christ. Franklyn told us of one man who had been executed, who went to his death singing worship songs, just like Stephen in the Bible.

Declaration for Australia
July

You are a country of many nations and have a varied heritage, which I value. Those who have owned the land for the longest time, My aboriginal people, have suffered much at the hands of those who invaded and plundered their lands. There has been some restoration, but I hold you accountable for any outstanding injustice.

Others came as punishment, often for menial crimes. They lost their families and were treated as slaves by those responsible for their 'rehabilitation'. The stoic resilience they needed to survive lives on in many of their descendants. Though it is made light of now, it is a sense of shame for the past.

I want to declare My *freedom* over you, whatever your origins may have been. You have a survivor's spirit and a pioneer's determination to make a future. I see this in the heart you have for the disadvantaged, the vulnerable, and the disenfranchised.

You love life and adventure. You are willing to take risks to achieve new things. I value these qualities in you and will use them for My Kingdom purposes.

Your forefathers also brought with them the traditions of Freemasonry, which are embedded in the foundations of this country. This is an abomination to Me and is demonic in its origins and practices. When you recognise and demolish this stronghold and acknowledge Me as Lord of the nation, I will bring blessing and joy to you. I call you to repent and turn away from these beliefs and practices. Then, you will fully enter your destiny as a nation and as individuals.

I want you to see yourselves as I see you, because I love you and will use your strength and tenacity, as you learn to trust Me. As you surrender to Me, I want to change your hearts so that you can be open to all I have given you. I want you to become more aware of and sensitive to My love and to experience the care I have for you as your heavenly Daddy.

Van Diemen's Land

On 5 July, we left for Tasmania. The Dutch explorer Abel Tasman was the first European to land on the shores of Tasmania in 1642. He was also the first European to discover New Zealand. Landing from the *Heemskerck* at Blackman's Bay and later having the Dutch flag flown at North Bay, Tasman named it Anthoonij van Diemenslandt, in honour of the governor-general of the Dutch East Indies, who had sent him on his voyage of discovery. Between 1772 and 1798, only the south-eastern portion of the island was visited. Tasmania was not known to be an island until the British navigators Matthew Flinders and George Bass sailed round it in the *Norfolk* in 1798 and 1799.

We flew into Hobart, the capital, and stayed for three nights which meant we were able to explore the surrounding area. Again, we had God's favour and we were offered a hire car; a Nissan X-Trail for only $20 a day, which was both an upgrade and a reduced fee.

Janet recalled that her aunt Beryl and uncle Arthur had arrived in Tasmania over sixty years previously, having emigrated with their six children on the *SS Arcadia*. After a six-week journey, it must have been a relief for them to arrive on dry land. We wondered how much had changed since then. Certainly, the Tasman Bridge was a new addition, spanning from North Hobart to the islands beyond.

With some trepidation, we decided to visit Port Arthur, which was one of the first places where Prisoners of Mother England, or 'Pommies', were incarcerated. Despite some damage from bush fires, it remains as a sobering memorial to our less attractive history of deporting 'criminals', often for stealing just a loaf of bread or a handkerchief. Some were as young as 9 years old, though this practice was later ended. Prisoners who were willing to learn were taught trades, which after their release gave them an opportunity to start afresh. We felt sorry for the soldiers and their families who were also forced to live there, as it was such an isolated community.

On our last day in Hobart, we drove up Mount Wellington, which is over 1 kilometre high and, at the time of our visit, the peak was above the clouds. There was even a bit of snow on the ground – in July!

Richmond (formerly Coaltown) has many original buildings from the nineteenth century, and it was easy to visualise how people used to live in those days.

On 8 July, we travelled south to the Huon Valley and to Geeveston, Australia's most southerly administrative centre. We had been invited to stay with Peter and Annie Cawthorn, who welcomed us into their home. It has a wonderful view overlooking the Huon River near the estuary which was a still, calm stretch of water when we were there.

The following day, we went to the Southwest Wilderness, another World Heritage site to tick off our list, and visited the Tahuna Forest Reserve. It is sad that in Tasmania there is so much evidence of roadkill. However, on our way to the Reserve, we saw a lovely group of lively wallabies and an echidna.

In the forest, an aerial walkway has been constructed so that visitors can climb up to 50 metres above the forest floor. This gave a unique perspective and we could see the tops of trees that had been growing for hundreds of years.

The colony of Van Diemen's Land was only a few years old when explorers first found ancient tree trunks buried in the mud of a river south-west of Hobart. It is considered to be the best pine in the southern hemisphere, it grows only 5 millimetres a year and has a resin which preserves it from rotting, even after felling and lying in water. Piners (men who went into the wilderness by river to cut the pine trees, up until forty years ago) risked life and limb to find these prized trees. Huon Pine may no longer be felled, but there is still plenty of wood, which can be collected from the rivers and sold in limited quantities.

Huon Pines!

On Sunday 10 July, we went to Dover Community Church, which is probably the most southerly church in Australia, and were invited to take the service for a congregation of around twenty-five people. We talked about our trip and involvement in Healing Rooms, and we prayed for those who came for healing.

Mining and Midwifery

Our journey continued and on 11 July, we left Geeveston. Leaving when we did was God-directed as there was severe flooding in this area a day or so after we left. This could have affected our travel.

The lush green scenery was impressive as we travelled over the mountains and through forests and valleys. But as we arrived in Queenstown, near the west coast, we felt there was great spiritual oppression on the area. It has become a virtual ghost-town, due to the closure of mining some years ago. In its heyday, the Mount Lyell gold and copper mining district had numerous smelting works, brick-works, and sawmills with a population of over 10,000. Today, less than 2,000 now remain.

We stayed at the once-impressive Empire Hotel. The 'Grand Old Lady of the West' is a Tasmanian icon and has a prominent facade in the town. It is rich in history, dating back to the wealth of the mining era at the turn of the twentieth century. Inside, guests are greeted by a beautifully handcrafted, National Trust listed, staircase made from Tasmanian Blackwood. Its sweeping bannisters were crafted in the UK then shipped out at the end of the nineteenth century when the hotel was first built.

We felt that God told us to leave early, and we later heard that severe snowfall had come to the area only two hours after we left – another example of our heavenly Father looking after us every day of our adventure.

We travelled north through Rosebery, where Janet's aunt and uncle had settled with their family all those years ago, and we were again aware that the town had 'lost its heart'. Very few people live there now and the few miners that remain commute in to work.

Arriving in Ulverstone, we were again struck by how many places in the former British Empire and colonies are named after towns and cities in the UK. Good friends of ours were for many years missionaries with Wycliffe Bible Translators, working in many countries including Mexico and North Africa. In their retirement, they chose to live in the delightful Lancastrian town of Ulverston.

Welcomed by Milton and Carolyn Smith, we later went to the Healing Rooms in the town and spent time with their team of around twelve people, sharing and praying with them.

Janet's cousin Trevor and his wife Glenda live in Wynyard, on the north coast. It was special to be with them again, as it had been ten years since we had seen them when they had last visited the UK. They live out in the country and have two sheep, a ram, two hens, and some ducks. During our stay with them, we explored more of the wilderness at Dip Falls, where the water cascades down a steep precipice. At the Falls, we saw the biggest diameter tree in Tasmania, a stringy bark pine. On a rather cloudy day we ventured up Cradle Mountain and saw the peak swathed in mist, but there were still people trudging off to camp and to try and find some snow for skiing.

On our way back, we went to Sheffield, a country town whose fortunes have been revived by the sixty enormous open-air murals around the town. These magnificent paintings trace the history of the town and celebrate the life of Gustav Weindorfer, a Cradle Mountain pioneer. Over 60,000 visitors come to view the paintings every year.

We also had an interesting visit to Wings Wildlife Park, where we saw a 'mob' of kangaroos, including one carrying a joey. They were so tame, we were able to feed and stroke them.

Our last day with Trevor and Glenda was quite eventful. After the morning service in the Lifehouse Church in Burnie, we drove around the area looking at over twenty homes in which Janet's aunt had lived – she did enjoy moving to new houses. We wondered whether she had issues with the taxman.

On our return, it soon became clear that one of Trevor's sheep was about to lamb. It was nearly dark when lamb number one emerged. Then it was number two's turn and its head popped out, but nothing more. By this time, it was dark. We were trying to see what was happening, running around the paddock with a torch. Finally, the sheep was coaxed into the lambing shed. Trevor and Glenda held her down while Janet was at the business end delivering the lamb. It was an interesting and exciting experience. The little black lamb (her sister who had arrived earlier was white) was doing well and Trevor and Glenda decided to name her Janet. Certainly, without her skills and timely intervention, all three animals would have died. So, we're not sure how we feel about Janet's namesake later becoming Sunday roast!

Seeing this new life gave us pause for thought for all those that God wants to bring to birth spiritually, and of our part in that whole process. Certainly, we have been delighted to be the 'midwives' at the time when people have been 'born-again'.

Our last few days in Tasmania were spent in Launceston (yes, just like in Cornwall), where we spent time with a group who were about to launch a Healing Rooms in the town. It was an awesome, stirring moment when one of the members called Beau blew the *shofar*.

On our last morning, we had time with our hosts, Steve and Victoria, and they shared a prophetic picture of us carrying Olympic torches wherever we went, taking God's light with us as we travelled.

MCG and Magnificent Treasure

Some say that 'men are from Mars and women are from Venus'. In our case, David prefers to read maps and Janet likes to ask for directions! GPS is an amazing invention, but in order for it to work, your information needs to be exact. On 20 July, we arrived at Melbourne Airport and jumped in our hire car. We eventually found our hotel after a slight diversion of 240 kilometres – all because we went to the wrong 'Barkly Road'.

The next day, we went to stay with Janet's cousin Bob and his wife Ann in their lovely home overlooking the city. Later, we drove to the Dandenong Ranges, up in the hills where people come in the summertime (which is in December) for picnics to escape the heat.

Stairway Healing Rooms in Vermont was like no other we have visited anywhere else in the world. Up to eighty people come for prayer one Saturday every month, and they have a team of over fifty people praying for them. There was even a band playing live worship music and others producing amazing prophetic paintings. Children are also part of the prayer team and are wonderfully used, especially in receiving pictures the Lord gives them for the visitors.

Before we left, a team member called Michelle shared a picture of us carrying a treasure chest, which was being filled up as we travelled around the world. The treasures were insights, wisdom and all the other things we were to discover on our trip – and they were for us to gather up and then to share with different people further down the line. It was most encouraging. We met later in the week with the director, Jenny Cornish and another team member, Maryann, and shared together at a coffee shop. We lost count of the amount of cups of coffee we drank during the year. You can imagine our amazement when Maryann said that she saw us carrying satchels of treasures to receive and give away.

On Sunday 23rd, we were taken by Bob to the world-famous MCG (Melbourne Cricket Ground) to watch his team, The Hawks, play Richmond in an AFL (Australian Football League) match. Fortunately, his team won. The rules seemed a bit rough and ready to us, with the objective of scoring tries achieved by wrestling the ball from the opposition – by almost any means possible – and then punting it as far up the field as possible.

We had a few moments of homesickness during the year, so our visit to our pastors' daughter Johanna and her husband Jon was delightful – once we found the right house. Once again, we had problems with our phones, so we did some door-knocking until one resident kindly searched Google and found the right house number on his laptop. It was wonderful to hear Johanna's English accent. At that time, she and her husband Jon lived in a part of Melbourne that has the feeling of a small village, with older terraced houses and little gardens. We later enjoyed seeing her wonderful art gallery.[4]

Spending some precious time with the teams of Geelong and Werribee Healing Rooms at director Gael Ranine's home for a joint meeting, we enjoyed praying for many of them. We were also given another prophetic picture of blue and green gems, which linked with the earlier pictures of treasure. Blue symbolises life and green stands for the Holy Spirit; we were being given life and growth. Later in the week, we visited the Geelong Healing Rooms and had some time to pray with the team and lead them in communion together. We joined the teams and prayed for about fifteen visitors. We later received some wonderful testimonies:

'My painful hip is healed! No more pain! Hallelujah!'

'A big thank you and glory to God. My husband received prayer on Friday for his knees and feet, and now he is pain-free and telling everybody he knows about his healing. He is also willing to come again!'

On Friday 26 July, we headed north-west to visit Janet's cousin Ray in the small town of Clunes, near Ballarat. He gave us an insight into the way of life in the outback. We were fascinated by the former gold-mining towns, now derelict, and other areas where people still go prospecting for gold. Ray was a bit disappointed when we didn't hire a metal detector to go digging for gold ourselves.

Worshipping at Ballarat Community Church on the Sunday we later explored the town. We enjoyed glorious sunshine as we wandered by a large lake which had been specially created for the water sports events in the 1956 Olympics.

---

4. www.johannawilbraham.co.uk

Friends Old and New

On 3 August, we were sad to say goodbye to Bob and Ann, before another flight – our thirteenth since we started. This time we were travelling from Melbourne to Port Macquarie via Sydney.

At Port Macquarie, we hired a car so that we could relish the coastal journey northwards. We were met by David Curtis, director of the Healing Rooms there. Exploring the area in the car as it was raining, we drove down to Crowdy Head, where there wasn't a soul in sight.

A special time was had meeting with the Healing Rooms team, seeing how they operated, and acquiring some more treasures for our chest. We also joined in praying for visitors and saw God healing, particularly in the area of emotional issues.

Our next port of call was Coffs Harbour, some two hours' drive north along the coast. We went to the home of Ray and Jan Beavis, who hosted us overnight, and there we met Sue Dalton who, along with Jan, are the directors of the Healing Rooms in the town. Their home overlooked the coast, giving us stunning views of the beach.

In the evening, we met at the Baptist church and worshipped God together, including dancing and waving flags. We also had an opportunity to pray for people to be healed. The next day, Sue collected us at 9.30 a.m. and took us on an astonishing tour of the area. With the Great Dividing Range in the background, we were able to see a variety of beautiful scenery, including bush and cultivated areas. Even in the winter, the land is lush and green. We followed the local coastline which has sandy beaches and rugged cliffs where the mountains join the sea. It was most captivating. We were glad of that brief snapshot before we had to leave to travel on to Byron Bay, which was a further three hours north.

Beach!

Byron Bay is quite an alternative city, where there is a large concentration of people espousing New Age beliefs and practices. We were keen to visit, having heard about the Healing Rooms there, run by Phil Mason, a former 'New Ager' who now also leads a Christian church called The  New Earth Tribe. Phil wrote the book *Quantum Glory*, which we had read prior to our departure from the UK. Certainly there were some pungent smells around from joss sticks and other things!

> *For example, he describes how, on one occasion at a New Age fair, they had a team of Christians at a booth set up to pray for healing, offer dream interpretation, prophecy, and Psalm readings. A woman passed by in obvious pain. One of the team offered to pray for her and she agreed. She had a piece of glass embedded in her foot, which could not be removed surgically as she would suffer nerve damage. After prayer, a piece of glass fell on the ground, which she confirmed had come from her foot. When she removed her shoe, sock and bandage, there was just a tiny scar where the glass had come out. She was healed and left rejoicing. With God nothing is impossible.*

Unfortunately, there was no Healing Rooms taking place while we were there, but we spent an hour with Robyn, one of the directors, who explained how they pray with anyone who comes, and always aim to avoid Christian jargon – quite a challenge! Phil presents in layman's terms the fact that God operates supernaturally

On 9 August, Janet went whale-watching: there was one pod of three whales consisting of mother, newborn whale (just under a week old), and 'escort' which is another whale who helps the mother protect her baby for the first few months. They were performing their moves for the awestruck sightseers and showing the young calf how to flip, dive, and leap in the water. She learned that whales are pregnant for a whole year – and they have her sympathy! They do, however, only have to look after their young for the first year, at which point their parenting responsibilities end. Not that Janet would have wanted to have had less time raising our family! In many ways, it passed all too quickly. We love you Paul, Mark, Chris and John, and now our three daughters-in-law and six grandchildren.

On 10 August, we arrived in Brisbane, the place where Janet's father emigrated to in the 1920s and was a jackaroo (an Australian cowboy) for several years before returning to the UK. On his return, he met Janet's mother, and the rest is history.

We stayed in the CBD, which meant we had easy access to the city. We discovered the area via the free city hopper, a ferry that takes people to destinations each side of the Brisbane River. The architecture was a mixture of old and new buildings and there was quite a lot of Art Deco to delight the eye.

We met with John and Merilyn Edwards, who have responsibility for Healing Rooms in Queensland and the whole Asia Pacific Division. Later, we were caught in a tropical downpour – this was a taste of things to come.

A couple of days later, we were able to spend some time with the rest of the team at Brisbane Healing Rooms, led by Barry and Lynette Howes, and we joined them as they prayed with visitors. A few days later, we spent an evening with the team. We did some teaching and prayed for them. We also spent some time at Chermside Healing Rooms, near Brisbane, and met Philip and Cynthia Deaner and some of their team.

One of the international languages is music. We enjoy a wide range of different styles and genres, and where possible we try to get to live performances. We enjoyed some jazz at a local club one Friday evening.

On Saturday 13 August, we got up at 5.30 a.m. to go on an adventure weekend to Moreton Island, which lies just off the coast of south-east Queensland. The Coral Sea lies on the east coast of the island. change to: Ninety-five per cent of the island is contained within a national park and is a popular destination for day-trippers, four-wheel drivers, campers, recreational anglers, and whale-watchers. Together with Fraser Island, Moreton Island forms the largest sand structure in the world. There are some extremely rare species of trees and plants to be found.

It was our compromise to visiting the Great Barrier Reef, which would have been too costly and time-consuming. We also had serious ethical issues about the environmental damage caused to the Reef by tourists. However, we had a great time. We were the oldest people on the trip and we opted for the hotel rather than camping in the somewhat decrepit tents. When we saw the spiders and the primitive conditions – only cold showers and toilets about 100 yards away in the bush – we were very pleased we had chosen modern accommodation.

Our weekend included going on safari in a four-wheel drive across the island, which is densely forested. We learned that a bush fire had destroyed all the trees and vegetation some time ago in the centre of the island, and it has never grown back. With a height of 90 metres and situated 280 metres above sea level, it is one of the highest sand dunes in the world. And guess what? We were able to slide down it!

Sand tobogganing consists of lying on a piece of waxed hardboard, either face-down or sitting. Then you slide down a hill, reaching speeds of up to 80 kilometres per hour. David stayed on his board the whole way but Janet came off about halfway down! Unfortunately, we have no pictures to prove it as the sand would have got into our camera. Janet decided to climb up and try again – slightly better the second time, but it was hard work climbing a 90-metre sand dune.

She also went snorkelling among the tropical fish and saw coral growing on some old ships that had been deliberately scuttled to provide an artificial reef. In the evening, Janet was able to feed a dolphin called Rani, the alpha male of a pod of wild dolphins that comes to be fed under close supervision at sunset every day. It was magical having them so near. Unfortunately, we weren't allowed to swim with them.

Early the next day, we were again collected by the four-wheel drive. The main highlights of this day included visiting Mount Tempest, the highest point on the island. We also went to the Blue Lagoon which was rather a muddy brown colour due to tea tree oil in the water. We discovered a Portuguese man-of-war jellyfish, with a string nearly five yards long, buried in the sand. Its venomous tentacles deliver a painful sting, which can be fatal – fortunately, no-one trod on it!

We packed our bags once again and left for Toowoomba to the home of Cec and Dianne Pedersen. David had previously met Cec through work at a conference in Malaysia. Their home was a forty-minute drive from Toowoomba and was a stark contrast to the city. All around us we could hear the beautiful sounds of the butcher birds. Their house was surrounded by gum trees and a colourful garden which Cec had been creating over two years since he had retired – it was idyllic!

We spent a week with them and their adopted daughters, Evie and Jenny, who had come from the Philippines (which would be our next port of call). They taught us about their national flag; that in times of peace the blue edge is at the top and in times of war, the red edge is at the top. Obviously, we were hoping to see blue on top when we arrived.

Cec took us to many beautiful places in the area, which had been devastated by flooding five years previously. There was also a redundant railway station called Spring Bluff, which has won prizes many times at the annual spring flower festival. We enjoyed their vibrant colours even in the winter

We drove around Lockyer Valley and visited Wyvenhoe Dam and some pioneer villages which were set up with buildings and equipment from 150 years ago – fascinating!

Toowoomba is a city 'set on a hill'.[5] The Great Dividing Range, or the Eastern Highlands, is Australia's largest mountain range. It is the third longest land-based range in the world. The range is 3,500 kilometres (2,175 miles) in length and runs along the whole east coast of Australia.

We explored Toowoomba and spent time with the Healing Rooms team there, headed up by Alan and Robyn Small, who also pastor the Range Christian Fellowship. We felt very welcome there and were involved in praying for visitors. One of these was an elderly gentleman, who shuffled into the prayer room very slowly using a walking frame, accompanied by his wife. He had lost most of the feeling down one side of his body and his speech was slurred. Clearly suffering from the effects of a stroke, he asked for Jesus to heal him. Janet discerned that he had been involved in Freemasonry. In addition to our prayers for healing, we ministered in the power of Jesus' name and through the blood He shed on the cross at Calvary against the effects of the occult. After just thirty minutes, the man walked out completely unaided.

---

5. Matthew 5:14

Earthquake!

On Sunday, we worshipped at the church. We talked about our journey and prayed with a number of people in the congregation.

> *While we were at the Range Healing Rooms, one of the leaders shared how God had recently woken her up and told her to gather a team of people to pray one Thursday, which was two days later. God had told her that an earthquake was expected in Toowoomba that day. They prayed for several hours, and later heard that there had indeed been an earthquake, but it had travelled further north and out into the ocean. If that earthquake had occurred in the city, many lives could have been lost and buildings demolished. God answers prayer because He cares about people.*

On 24 August we headed back to Brisbane to catch our plane to Sydney for our last week in Australia. On arrival, we hired a car – another free upgrade – and travelled south to stay with Ursula Roulston in Nowra.

At that time, Ursula was the director of a Healing Rooms in a room at the rear of her house. We had some special prayer time with her team. We then travelled back to Sydney and met again with Franklyn and Dianne Elliot, who gave us a further tour, including seeing the Blue Mountains. We saw the 'Three Sisters' and looked across the valley over a forest of eucalyptus trees. The deep blue colour of the mountains is caused by the vapour from the eucalyptus trees and we could smell it too. It would certainly clear any blocked noses!

We also visited an opulent Art Deco hotel called The Majestic, which has been beautifully restored and has peacock feathers edging the curtains – poor peacocks!

In the UK, we often take the NHS for granted. While we were away, we needed to stock up on enough anti-malarial tablets for the remainder of our trip and had to get all the right documents from the Australian Department of Health. Then we were required to register with an appropriate family physician. Finally, we presented our prescription to an authorised pharmacist, but they didn't have enough tablets in stock, so we returned the following day. The boxes seemed to take up a huge amount of space in our suitcases. David also insisted on having all the right paperwork, duly stamped, in case we were stopped by an overly vigilant officer somewhere in rural Asia.

On our final day in Sydney, we had a marvellous tour of Sydney Opera House. It is an awesome structure. Some of the facts we were given include:

- It was designed by Jorn Utzon who was only paid £5,000 for the design

- It should have taken four years to build, but instead it took fourteen

- It was opened in 1973 by the Queen

- The roof is designed to look like the sails of a ship

- If all the sails were fitted together, they would make a perfect sphere

- There are 1,056,006 tiles on the sails and they aren't white because that would be too dazzling!

It is certainly worth a visit if you go 'down under'.

Mileage

In the first six months of our trip we travelled:

- 13,000 miles by plane
- Over 5,000 miles by car
- 2,000 miles by train
- Plus, the various side-trips on buses, ferries and boats

We have slept in 51 different beds for differing lengths of time. We have used a wide variety of toilets – we don't know how many, but we encountered some unusual ones. Our smallest hotel room was the 'pod-pad' in Christchurch, which had a king-size bed that occupied over half the space. Our favourite hotel was the Capri in Brisbane, with fantastic facilities including a gym and large swimming pool. Our least favourite was probably The Shakespeare in Auckland, New Zealand, mainly because we were on the top floor and had to climb 90 stairs to get to our room.

At this point, we were halfway through our adventure. Our next stop was Asia, where the fun really was about to begin.

CHAPTER FOUR

The Uttermost Parts of the Earth

September

Our journey from Sydney to the Philippines began on 1 September when we flew via Kuala Lumpur to Manila, on the main island of Luzon, one of more than 7,000 islands that make up the Philippines.

We arrived at the airport to the strains of *'Dashing through the snow'*, which we thought was a little early! We later learned that Filipinos love Christmas and celebrate it throughout the '-ber' months. This includes being serenaded by Christmas songs in almost every public place from September onwards and Christmas decorations are on display everywhere. We didn't see any Christmas cards with snow and robins though.

The climate was hot and humid, between 30 – 32°C, though in the hot season of May and June it is often above 40°C! Our first hotel was in the CBD (central business district) and the air conditioning was wonderful.

We soon became aware of the huge contrasts in living conditions. Our first taxi journey from the airport gave us glimpses of abject poverty; homes constructed out of discarded refuse and families living under motorway fly-overs. There were children being bathed in the river and fountains, and others as young as our own grandchildren were dashing between the traffic, hoping to receive money or food.

The next day, we explored the area and were relieved to discover the air-conditioned Manila Hotel; a magnificent iconic structure built in 1912, with employees graded according to the grandeur of their uniform. We later travelled by horse and carriage to visit the Intra Muros or Walled City, the oldest part of Manila, with buildings dating from the early nineteenth century, as well as relics from the Japanese occupation of the Philippines. Such dramatic contrasts of living conditions, and smells, and colours, and sounds was to become a permanent feature of our time in the Far East. Heart-rending poverty was evident everywhere, and in close proximity to many who lived in relative luxury. We gained a greater understanding of our Lord's passion for the poor.

Our senses were constantly bombarded with a rich diversity of all that is exotic and wonderful. The normal hustle and bustle of everyday life in any city these days was made even more pronounced in those in South East Asia by the incredible sights and sounds and smells that assaulted us on every corner. The new, the strange, and the bizarre would often become the norm.

Declaration for the Philippines

September

My precious Filipino people, I love you. I love your warmth, your gentle spirit, your desire to please, your vivacity, your desire for peace. Over many centuries, you have suffered invasions and others imposing their rules and ideologies upon you.

I have a plan for you My people. I have heard the cry of those who already seek My face. I will bless you and you will see My Spirit moving in the nation more powerfully than ever before. You will see My Spirit poured out in such measure in these days. It will be like your monsoon rains. I will soak you, I will drench you, I will cleanse you, I will refill you so that you will overflow with My living water into your communities and nation. I want to transform you from the inside out, then you will see My Kingdom come in the Philippines, as it is in Heaven.

In these days I am calling all who love and acknowledge My name to come before Me; to humble yourselves and pray, and seek My face, to turn from your wicked ways.

Then My promise to you is, 'I will hear from heaven, I will forgive your sin, and I will heal your land' (2 Chronicles 7:14).

I am calling all Christian leaders to seek My face and pray. It is not about your authority, power, or control, but as you lead by example you will call your congregations to come before Me in repentance and to pray for your people together. Then you will see this outpouring that will transform your nation.

I am also calling you to show My love in practical ways, providing for the poor, the needy, the vulnerable, the outcast and the addicted in your community. I will bring them freedom and hope, as a demonstration of My love, My provision and My healing power.

On Sunday 4th, we met Roy Carandang, the national director of Healing Rooms in the Philippines. He collected us at 7.15 a.m. and brought us to his church in Las Piñas, which was not far away to the south of Manila, but took over forty minutes in the heavy traffic.

Roy is the pastor of a church which occupies buildings that used to be part of a luxurious hotel complex, but which had been abandoned and fallen into disrepair. The church had deliberately moved there to be nearer the poor of the area. The congregation has been gradually renovating the buildings. In addition to the church, they run a preschool and primary and secondary schools. They also have arts, drama, and music departments.

We visited an area nearby known as 'The Lagoon' (filthy swamp!), where families dwell in homes constructed of whatever materials they can find – plastic sacks, metal, wood – and which are frequently flooded, especially in monsoon season. Later in our visit, three young lads from the village gave us an impromptu violin recital of a traditional Spanish piece which they played to a very high standard. The boys' music will provide a passport to the city music academy and this will offer them a better future.

In many ways, the Sunday service at the church mirrored our own experience in Havant, with its focus on worship, teaching and relationships. We were welcomed into that part of the family of God and felt really at home.

After the service, we were able to pray for many who needed healing, and we later had lunch with Roy, his wife Adora and children Tim, Tobia and Katrina. We learned that family, food and photographs are an important part of life in the Philippines. Roy also shared what he sensed was part of God's purpose for our coming to these islands, which may be more significant than we had thought.

On 5 September, we visited CRIBS Foundation, Inc.[6] which was the first orphanage opened in the Philippines some forty-two years ago by two Christian women. When we had previously been in Australia staying with Cec and Dianne, we learnt that their adopted daughters Evie and Jenny had been rescued as little girls by CRIBS when their mother could no longer care for them. Although it had been thirteen years since they had been adopted, some of the staff at the orphanage still remembered them and were delighted to see photos of them as young adults. They were in tears as they could see photos of how the two girls had grown into lively, intelligent, healthy teenagers with a zest for life. It wasn't often that they were able to see fruit of their good work. But it was also sobering to witness that the orphanage now also provides a home for a number of young teenagers who have been trafficked into sexual abuse.

Another significant issue in the nation, which has been receiving international attention, is the action being taken against drug-trafficking and abuse. President Duterte had only been in office a few months and had stated his determination to rid the nation of this destructive problem. His methods raised criticism, but the problem is endemic, with more than 1 million addicts in a population of just over 100 million. Church leaders and pastors have been asked to help in the challenging task of rehabilitating the hundreds of thousands of 'surrenderees' – those who have come forward asking for help.

Healing Rooms ministry is held in high regard in the Philippines and the local government units (LGU) would like one in each of their forty thousand 'barangays' (wards) – quite a challenge!

We are in contact with Dr Graham Giles in the UK who has a special electronic device[7] which can help to facilitate

---

6. www.cribsfoundation.com
7. www.spera.digital

recovery from addiction. With the contacts we have made in the Philippines, it could well be used there and become a significant part of dealing with this huge problem.

We had the privilege of meeting BG (he told us his real name was unpronounceable) and his wife Jhoey, Christians who integrate their faith with their work. As a graphic designer, BG had recently redesigned the country's paper currency and on every note, in almost invisible writing he included the words, 'blessed is the nation whose God is the Lord'. Because of the extremely high standards and quality of his work, he was later asked to redesign their national passport, when he also took the opportunity to include other Scriptures.

After our first week, we moved to the church's mission house, a property owned by Roy and Adora and located near the church. This made getting around much easier. However, the mission house lacked most amenities, and so after a couple of days we moved into the Vivere building where Roy owns a very up-market condominium on the sixteenth floor with magnificent views of the city. We gasped at the panoramic views.

We met with people in the church on a weeknight meeting, as well as on Sunday. Over the weeks, we developed a close relationship with the church, whose members were mostly locals, including parents whose children attended the school run by the church. On our last Sunday there, we were told that we were now honorary 'Nanei' (Grandma) and 'Tatei' (Grandpa)! We were touched by their acceptance of us as family after such a short time.

Transport in the Philippines

During our visit, we travelled by many different means – taxi, car, horse and carriage. We even used a tricycle; a motorbike with an improvised sidecar attached. This could accommodate four or more people depending on the size of their posteriors and whether they were happy to ride pillion and without a helmet. We surprised many people by being willing to travel in the Jeepney, originally a GP (government property) transport vehicle left behind by the American soldiers after the Second World War, which has been modified and adapted so that it can seat more than twenty people. These are incredibly colourful and cheap, but you have to know which route you need and when to get off. We only used these when we were with people who knew where they were going. Fares were passed forward to the driver and change was passed back by the other passengers.

Food

We tried many Filipino dishes and generally liked them. They eat a lot of beef, pork, and fish and we enjoyed lapu-lapu, as well as mullet and a range of shellfish. They also love their desserts, so David was happy! Food tends to be ordered by the group and then the dishes are shared so that everyone can have a taste. They also have some amazing fruits:

- Jackfruit – grows as a very large light green fruit, which tastes similar to mango and peach. You buy a chunk which is then cut up and put in a plastic box

- Rambutan – has a hairy red shell. Inside it looks a bit like a lychee or grape but tastes more like pear

- Mangosteen – purple in colour, good for the immune system, taste is a cross between a melon, a lychee and a soft banana

- Guyabano – soursop, small green bumpy fruit, which makes a delicious drink, tasting like a combination of strawberry and pineapple

- Pomelo – like a large, pink grapefruit but sweeter

- Lanzones – look like small, new potatoes until you peel off the skin, and the taste can vary from tart to sweet, like grapes

- Dragon fruit – which is usually a bright red oval-shaped ball with spikes, and has a mild flavour like kiwi fruit

- Durien – the smelliest fruit in the world, not allowed to be brought on public transport or into hotels!!

Visits

Roy took us to see Taal volcano. It is the smallest volcano in the world and is situated on the outskirts of Manila. It is an extinct volcano and the crater is now filled with water, with an island situated in the middle. We also had a day out at Villa Escudero, which was originally owned by a Spanish family and is now a fascinating place to visit and explore; it has swimming pools and you have the opportunity to eat lunch with your feet in the river. There is an amazing exhibition of dance and culture which has been developed down the centuries as a result of the indigenous, Islamic, and Spanish influences.

On another memorable day, we visited a branch of Iris Ministries,[8] which is part of the outreach to the poor started by Heidi Baker in Mozambique.

The local mission team lives in a part of the capital called Tondo, where the Smokey Mountain rubbish dump once existed. Blocks of housing were built to accommodate those who used to live on the dump. But the overcrowding, dirt and squalor of the former living conditions has only been replaced with vertical blocks of similar squalor.

---

8. www.irisglobal.org/philippines/about

Iris Ministries is based in a tiny apartment among the people. Three young women there have committed themselves to reach out to the poor, both practically and with God's love.

We were invited to join them as they visited a maternity ward in the local public hospital. We were surprised and upset to see that in the maternity ward there were ten beds, and twenty mothers! The mattresses and sheets were filthy. A number of babies had blood infections and two of the young women, who had just had stillbirths, had to be in the same ward. We were asked to pray for all the mothers and their babies, who were mostly Muslim.

> *One first-time mother had lost a lot of blood during the birth and had been waiting for a blood transfusion for three days because they had none of her blood group (B-positive) available. David clearly heard God say to him, 'Be positive'. David told the young woman that Jesus loved her so much that He gave His blood for her when He died on the cross. She was clearly moved by such news. David was then prompted by Jesus to follow His example, and offered to donate his blood for her, as he happens to be B-positive too. We headed to the blood donor department but unfortunately, David was refused as he was too old. When we returned to the ward, we were worried the young mother would be disappointed. Instead, she was overwhelmed; she couldn't believe that David cared enough to do this for her and, there and then, she decided to give her heart and life to Jesus and to become a Christian.*

On our second weekend, we flew to Cebu to meet Nicola Tancock. It had been sixteen years since we had seen her at our former church in London. Over the last few years, Nicola has worked for Christian organisations in Toronto, the UK, Australia, and now in the Philippines. She is youth pastor at a church in Lapu-Lapu on Cebu, which serves the community by running a primary school for local children. She also coordinates a small sewing factory, which helps to provide employment for local women. She has also helped to set up a similar sewing factory in India, and the proceeds from the business go to feed the poor and help trafficked young women.[9]

The weekend before we left the Philippines, we were invited back to speak at the 28th anniversary of their church. It was a joyful occasion.

We had been looking forward to visiting Palawan – an island where there is a newly registered World Heritage site called the Underground River. Travelling by coach took about two hours, during which time we had the unusual experience of listening to five Catholic nuns recite their morning prayers, ending with an impressive rendition of 'Ave Maria'!

We were taken by outrigger to the entrance of the river, which runs for several kilometres under the headland. Only torchlight is permitted due to the fact that it is home to several million bats and some rare aquatic creatures. There are also amazing limestone rock formations described as 'the Holy Family', 'Jesus', and 'the Virgin Mary', as well as a variety of fruits and vegetables. We were given some important advice: 'Keep your mouth shut when looking up in case the bats pee!'

On returning to the main island of Luzon, we had an unexpected meeting with one of the local mayors, who was known to Roy. We were ushered into his office and introduced

---

9.   https://www.spiritedclothes.co.uk/

as visitors from the UK. We chatted and then offered to pray with him. He seemed pleased to be asked, but before we started to pray, and as a mark of respect, he proceeded to remove his gun and holster! He was grateful since, along with all the other mayors, he had received a mandate from the president to restore law and order, but with few resources to help him. What a privilege that we could ask God to give him wisdom and direction in all his decision-making. It seemed likely that we would return to the Philippines before we travelled home via Israel.

CHAPTER FIVE

Bali and Bibles

October

It was a long, twelve-hour flight from Manila, Philippines to Bali, Indonesia, as it was a lot cheaper for us to go via Kuala Lumpur, Malaysia. We had our first experience of dinner being served for breakfast en route.

We decided it was time to have some R & R, so after quite a busy time in the Philippines, it was wonderful just to *be* for a few days. We were picked up from the airport by a special car and taken to Nusa Dua (two islands).

Whilst in Melbourne, David had found an amazing deal for a week's stay at the Mulia Resort.[10] On more than one occasion, it has been awarded the coveted title of *'The best hotel and resort in the world'*. It was breath-taking and so exotic. There was marble everywhere.

There were five pools to choose from and at least six restaurants, offering everything from traditional cuisine to Japanese, Chinese, Balinese, and Indonesian foods.

Humidity seemed as if it was at 100 per cent. It was like it had been in the Philippines and still just as hot, so our room was an air-conditioned haven. As you may remember, we were

---

10. www.themulia.com/bali-resort/

making observations of loos all over the world, and this would rate as the perfect ten. There was no handle for the flush, but instead a choice of about ten buttons – we just had to be careful which one we chose! The toilet seat cover rises as you open the door and closes when you're done. So, ladies, no more having to lower the heated seat after your spouse!

There seemed to be members of staff placed strategically wherever we went, to help us if we needed it. We discovered that 'Mulia' is Indonesian for 'majesty' – we guessed it was fit for King David and Queen Janet!

After eight days, we reluctantly left for our next hostelry, which was decidedly more downmarket but no less pleasant. The whole thing could have fitted into the Mulia's lobby area several times over. It had its own tiny swimming pool in the garden and it was much nearer for us to go for breakfast.

Surprisingly, since Indonesia has the largest Muslim population in the world, Bali seems to have a predominance of Hindu worshippers.

Transport in South East Asia is dominated by thousands of motorbikes. It is the preferred method of travel if you don't have a car and it is probably quicker. So we enjoyed a daytrip in our landlord's taxi and he drove us to a number of different places around the island. This included visiting a Barong, which is a dance and music performance telling a mythological tale about the battle between good and evil; how good triumphs in the end, and how redemption is achieved. As Christians, we know this is true, although our focus is on Jesus as our Redeemer.

It was also interesting to see that a large number of Muslim young people attended the performance on a school outing, bearing in mind that the story is rooted in Hindu culture. We learnt that Muslims and Hindus generally live quite peacefully together in Bali. Conversations with taxi drivers and other local people revealed a real culture of fear and the need to appease all the various gods by offerings of flowers, food and incense left outside homes and businesses. We felt quite sad that they live in dread of bad things happening, instead of having a relationship with the loving God who created the things they worship.

On this daytrip to Ubud we had Luwak coffee – the most expensive in the world. This is unique to Indonesia, though it is exported abroad. The coffee berries are fed to civets, then the bean seeds are extracted from their digested remains and processed into coffee – yum! It certainly tasted stronger than our normal instant brand. Fortunately, there were no after-effects!

On our first two Sundays in Indonesia, we fellowshipped in a local community church attended by expats as well as local people. After ten days, we still had no plans or direction from God. We were wondering whether we should consider exploring other parts of Indonesia, which has more than 17,000 islands stretching along the equator – from Papua New Guinea, just north of Australia, to Batam near Singapore. We still had not heard from the few contacts we had been given.

God had promised to guide us every step of our adventure, so on 12 October, we asked some friends to pray. It was quite incredible that within a couple of hours of sending our email, we had a response from Wahyudi, the director for Healing Rooms in Indonesia. He had been away on a trip and had not been online for a while but felt a prompt from Jesus to check his emails and contacted us immediately. That was quite a reminder for us to trust and pray.

The next day we met Wahyudi and established a wonderful rapport with him. And by the following day, he had brought us to his home, where we stayed in their delightful guesthouse.

We also met Eddy and his wife Phoebe. God uses Eddy in an extraordinary way to speak prophetically into people's lives.

God confirmed that we should accompany a team who were going to run some Healing Rooms training in Bandung, near Jakarta, and then join them on a mission trip to another island called Ambon. We were also awed when he described the route we were to follow after we had left the Philippines, which was our planned itinerary, and no one had been told beforehand. It certainly reinforced our confidence that we were following God's directions. All this took place on 13 October which is David's birthday – what a birthday present!

On 15 October, we flew to Bandung and were met by a Christian businessman who is a millionaire. He took us to the local bread factory which he owns. He and his wife were gentle, humble people whom God has entrusted with great wealth – after a lot of hard work. He now has over fifty factories throughout Indonesia, with over 6,000 employees. We were shown around the production line of the factory in Bandung. David had discussions with the owner about his business and was delighted to learn that although he had never been to university, he had learned everything he knew from 'the school of hard knocks'. The quality of his products and the excellence of his business practices testified to God's wonderful provision.

He and his wife invited us to stay at their beautiful mansion for the weekend and blessed us with a very large, and wholly unexpected, financial gift. We were reminded that God had promised to provide for all our needs. In hindsight, as we are now writing this on our return, we have seen how the total costs for the whole adventure were miraculously met in full.

One of the many people we were asked to pray for was a gentleman who was virtually bed-ridden because of severe complicated problems with his leg. After prayer, God completely healed him!

Declaration for Indonesia
October

I am calling My people in these islands; I am calling My people in these islands in these days; I am calling My people in these islands in these days to come together, to seek My face, to declare My presence, My Lordship in the land.

These islands of Indonesia are Mine. I created them long ago. My name will be declared and honoured across this nation. For too long, My enemy has held sway here. Much blood has been shed, but My blood was shed for you, to heal, forgive, cleanse, to renew. No one is excluded. My death on the cross and resurrection paid the price of your freedom and forgiveness.

Sound the trumpet!

Sound the *shofar*!

Declare My Lordship!

I am coming! I am coming to claim My land, My people.

I am coming to restore what has been stolen, what has been killed, what has been destroyed.

Put on your armour My people! Each piece in order.

The belt of truth – I am the only Way.

The breastplate of righteousness – I have covered your sin with My forgiveness.

The shoes of the gospel of peace – Take My message of love wherever you go.

The shield of faith – Trust in Me alone, when the enemy's arrows try to find their mark.

The helmet of salvation – Know whose you are and who you are. You are saved by grace.

The sword of the Spirit – This powerful weapon is all you need to defeat the enemy. My Word is enough.

Stand in this armour. Pray continually in the Spirit, and you will see breakthrough in this nation.

I love the people of these islands. My light comes to dispel the darkness, to show you who I am, to bring you the hope, destiny and purpose I have planned for you as individuals and as a nation.

Whilst in Bandung, we were also introduced to some more significant contacts who later helped us with our ongoing itinerary. One of these contacts was Larry, who contributed to a book we had read two years beforehand called, *A Wind in the House of Islam*. This well-researched paperback was based on over 1,000 interviews with people who had converted to Christianity in all the Islamic nations of the world. Apparently, half of them had received direct, personal, dreams or visions of Jesus, and the other half had been miraculously healed. They all had wonderful testimonies of encounters with the living, risen Christ.

On Sunday 16th, we attended the church in Bandung, which has so many members they have five services with over 800 people at each service. It was uplifting to be in a megachurch in the nation with the most Muslims in the world.

The following day began early, as we needed to prepare for the training which began at 8.30 a.m. Days tend to start early in the Far East to make the most of the cooler hours, though it's still around 28°C!

David has probably undertaken 'train the trainer' programmes for over 8,000 people in his career, and yet he was so impressed by the standard of training delivered by Yudi. He has had no formal training in teaching, but he did an amazing job, inspired by the Holy Spirit. Over eighty people of all ages attended the training course and a large number of these were young people. They were all passionate about being equipped to minister healing in their communities. Apart from briefly introducing ourselves and David sharing his experience of being healed, we were mostly there in a supporting role, partly because we don't speak Indonesian. We learned and prayed during the day and were humbled by what we experienced.

We saw a moving video clip about a father who was a bridge operator on the railway, who had to choose between sacrificing his son's life or saving the lives of a trainload of passengers. This reminded us of God's choice in sending His son Jesus to save us.[11]

We also saw a powerful yet harrowing depiction of Jesus' suffering at the crucifixion. It showed everybody present what it was like when Jesus experienced the weight of all the wrong things that have ever happened, as He took our place and took the weight of our sins on Himself and was judged by God.

The following morning, we got up at 4 a.m. and were fed some beef stew. Then we prepared to fly to Ambon, an island in the Maluku Islands, where the next training was to take place. As we left the airport in Ambon, we were accosted by a policeman, demanding to see our passports and visas. It was a bit intimidating and we were grateful that we had Yudi with us to help with communication. We later heard that not many foreigners visit there, and they can be treated with suspicion. Corruption and bribery are very common. God redeemed the situation later in the trip when were able to chat about Jesus with a security guard, a policeman, and a military policeman as we waited for a ferry.

Spiritual gateways are often contested. We learned that Ambon – part of the famous Spice Islands – was the place where Christianity first came to Indonesia in the 1500s by Portuguese, Dutch, and English traders who brought back the spices produced there. The backstory from the late 1990s told how there was a lot of bloodshed in a civil war between Muslims and Christians, where there were faults on both sides. It was perhaps not religious hatred but a corrupt civil service that sparked the carnage. It is sad that the only way they have been able to keep people safe is to segregate them into different geographical locations and to have a number of military barracks placed strategically on the island. We felt strongly

---

11. https://www.youtube.com/watch?v=_oZYi1j_Z8g

that there needed to be a release of forgiveness on both sides and ways found for them to live together in peace. Some of those who were affected by this past had specifically invited Yudi to come and they were very active in showing God's love to the community, regardless of religious affiliations.

The training again went well, apart from some power supply problems at key moments. The week continued with many visits to people's homes to pray for and encourage them. We were able to be involved when there was someone available to interpret.

One day, we got up at 5.30 a.m. and travelled to a smaller island called Seram, where we were driven at breakneck speed for over two hours to another town. We went to an Assemblies of God church to deliver some Indonesian Bibles and visited some local people to pray with them. Pantheism, Animism, and Paganism are rife in the area. Syncretism is a major problem for the local Christian pastors.

The return drive to the ferry was even more hair-raising as we travelled through monsoon rain lashing down. We were thankful to arrive safely at the ferry, and finally returned to our hotel at 10.30 p.m.

The next day, we decided to rest and enjoy the facilities in the hotel. After all, we were the oldest people on the team! Our return to Bali via Makassar went smoothly, though we had travelled in and out of time zones and weren't too sure what time it was when we arrived. On our last full day in Indonesia, we went to Bali Bird Park.

By this point in our journey, we had:

- Slept in 63 different beds

- Travelled on 30 planes

- And visited hundreds of different loos, ranging from a score of one to a perfect ten!

We had made friends with so many people across the nations, confirming what we already knew and believed – that basically all people have the same needs and passions and you can make friends even when you only have a few words that you understand in each other's language.

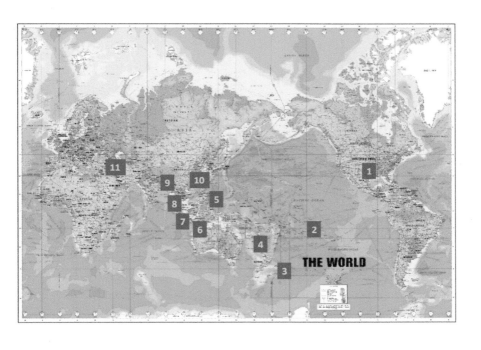

1. USA

2. Tahiti

3. New Zealand

4. Australia

5. Philippines

6. Indonesia

7. Singapore

8. Malaysia

9. Thailand

10. Vietnam

11. Israel

Us celebrating our 40th wedding anniversary in Kuala Lumpur

"As you go, proclaim this message:
'The kingdom of heaven has come near.'
Heal the sick, raise the dead, cleanse those
who have leprosy, drive out demons.
Freely you have received; freely give."

Matthew 10:7-8

Our mandate for a year's adventure with Jesus

Liberty!

David and Felix in Boise, Idaho, on Good Friday

Tahiti

Baptism at Snell's Bay, New Zealand

Queenstown, New Zealand

Janet delivering a baby lamb, Tasmania

Pastor Roy and the Church near Manila, Philippines

Slum dwellings near the church in Manilla, Philippines

Traditional dancers, Philippines

Ministry in Tondo, Philippines

Ambon, Indonesia

Penang, Malaysia

Old Town Phuket, Thailand

New Zealanders on mission to Chiang Mai, Thailand

Parasol factory, near Chiang Mai, Thailand

Hanoi, Vietnam

Bible study, Vietnam

Wedding day worship, Vietnam

Jerusalem, Israel

Nazareth, Israel

Tabernacle, Negev Desert, Israel

CHAPTER SIX

Bright Lights and Healings

November

Our stay in Singapore was a mere ten days. Singapore is an intriguing country. It means 'land of the lion' and it has a unique feel to it. We were aware of the links with the UK and its colonial past. There are many buildings from that era which have been restored or maintained. We had the opportunity to visit an exclusive gentlemen's club – now open to ladies too – called The Tanglin Club. It had amazing interior decor and so many restaurants – it was very grand! Our hosts, Dr Chan and his wife, had only said they would take us out for a Chinese meal. We were glad that we happened to be suitably dressed for our surroundings!

Singapore is a country situated mostly on one island at the southern end of the Malaysian peninsula and therefore land is at a premium. There is virtually no space for any farming, apart from growing vegetables in an artificial factory environment. Everything is imported.

As far as cuisine is concerned, you can find most eastern diets represented – Chinese, Japanese, Indonesian, Thai, and their own various blends of these. Janet was improving on her chopstick skills, though we found that in Indonesia and Singapore knives were rarely offered, even when you were eating large pieces of meat or fish. It's amazing how you learn what the protocol is by watching how your hosts tackle things.

Declaration for Singapore
November

Singapore – Land of the lion, you are a strategic nation in My purposes. As with so many countries, you have experienced much suffering and loss in your history. I have blessed you greatly over more recent years. I have entrusted you with wealth, stability, security and stature among the nations. I love you Singapore, land of many ethnicities. You have learned to live together peacefully and respectfully, and I honour you for that as many of your neighbours treat you with renown.

My heart for you as a nation is for you to recognise and receive My love for you. I have plans for you beyond your material success. But, as with My Laodicean church, 'You say, "I am rich; I have acquired wealth and do not need a thing.' But you do not realise that you are wretched, pitiful, poor, blind, and naked. I counsel you to buy from Me gold refined in the fire, so you can become rich; and white clothes to wear, so you can cover your shameful nakedness; and salve to put on your eyes, so you can see' (Revelation 3:17-18).

I have made you a centre of significance – politically, geographically, and commercially. Your economic importance is far greater than your size. But you are the hub and not the wheel. You have forgotten, like Corinth of old, to focus on Me and to put your trust in Me. I see beneath your veneer.

As you humble yourselves before Me, and like King Solomon acknowledge your need for My wisdom and direction for you as a nation in the coming days, I will bless you with even greater influence among the nations. You will be not only a financial hub, an example in how to provide economically and developmentally. But most of all with Me at the centre of all your plans, you will bring My love to those who come to you, and I will send you to those who have not yet heard the Good News of My love for them.

Visiting Singapore, as with parts of neighbouring Indonesia, was meaningful for David, as his father John had served in the Royal Marines during the Second World War. He knows John was stationed in Singapore and Java, though he has no further information. As with so many who went to war, his father never talked about it. Revisiting Singapore, and later Malaka and Penang in Malaysia became times of healing for him.

The day after we arrived in Singapore, we went back to Indonesia, by visiting a small offshore island. It was quite shocking to experience the differences in lifestyle, culture and poverty, after such a short journey. We had contact with an American couple, Jean and Dave, who have been serving as missionaries on Batam Island, which is just a one-hour boat ride from Singapore and is the most westerly island in Indonesia. They have developed a healing approach which helps people address unresolved issues in their lives and they have translated their resource materials into Indonesian.

We also made a trip to Sentosa Island – now a resort offering a Disneyland-type experience for families. It also has cable cars that take you high over the harbour to the mainland and give an amazing perspective. David reflected how different it would have looked seventy or so years ago – instead of over sixty cargo ships, cruise liners and luxury boats, the harbour would have been ablaze with burning vessels. A solemn recollection.

In Singapore, we were invited to visit three of the four Healing Rooms operating there. We found some differences as the basic model is adapted to the local culture and to some extent reflects the style of those in charge.

We were also privileged to meet Thio Gim Bok and his wife Thio Su Mien. We learned that in Singapore, the surname comes first. They are an amazing couple and we were given a copy of a book written by Su Mien detailing the astounding ways she has been led to pray for nations through what God has shown her about their history. It included an account of her niece, who had been declared brainstem dead. The doctors had wanted to switch off her life-support but after much prayer, she was completely restored to full health. The doctors said it had never happened before and it was all over the press in Singapore. The day of miracles is not over.

We asked for Gim Lok and Su Mien's support and counsel as we continued to pray for the nations we visited. They also started Healing Rooms in Malaysia in 2003, only a short while after they both became Christians.

During our stay we were also able to meet up with our friends from the Philippines – Roy, Adora, BG and Jhoey, and their families – who had come to attend a conference called 'Luminocity', which was established to encourage young Christian entrepreneurs to begin businesses based on Christian ethics and principles. It was special to reconnect with them and update them on our adventures.

We also recognised afresh that as we met national leaders of Healing Rooms in the Philippines, Indonesia, and Singapore, we have a role in helping to connect them with each other. They are now actively considering the possibility of an Asian Healing Rooms conference for these nations and maybe Thailand and Malaysia too.

Other special times here included visiting the Aquarium on Sentosa Island, which has everything from seahorses to sharks. The Bay Gardens, with their enclosed domes featuring flora from the five continents, was also an amazing experience, seeing the exotic birds flying freely within the huge enclosure. Janet encountered one parrot very closely.

Next stop was Kuala Lumpur.

Deeper into Asia

Time passes quickly when you are having fun! On Thursday 8 December, we arrived in Malaysia by coach. It cost a mere £10 each to travel for five hours from Singapore to Kuala Lumpur. It was so easy and a nice change from airports and everything associated with flying. It didn't take that much longer when you take into account the pre-flight check-in time, passport control, waiting for your luggage on arrival and then travelling from the airport to the city centre.

Reviewing the four weeks we spent in Malaysia would obviously include our 40th wedding anniversary, a high point in more ways than one, as we had our celebratory meal thirty-two floors up in an exclusive French restaurant overlooking Kuala Lumpur's 'Twin Towers'.

During our stay in Malaysia, we explored Kuala Lumpur, doing a 'hop-on-hop-off' trip around the city to visit various landmarks, including the Malaysian National Museum. This gave us some sense of the nation's history which although relatively peaceful now, has known great conflict in the past, with invasions by the Portuguese, Dutch, Japanese, and of course, the Brits.

Very self-conscious about our colonial heritage, and the harm done to so many nations by our forebears, we often apologised on their behalf to so many people. However, as in many places, the people we met spoke warmly of Britain's contribution in establishing their legal, educational, and political systems and good road networks. They also told us the importance of the English language, which is a passport for many to good job prospects in both Malaysia and abroad. It was sad to hear that there had been terrible conflict between Christians and Muslims as recently as 1999, when the river in Kuala Lumpur ran red with the blood of so many who died.

We enjoyed seeing the national flower Hibiscus *rosa-sinensis*, growing wild and in abundance. The flowers which for us are exotic, surviving only under special care, thrive in the wild along the roads.

Malaysia is a multicultural society, with many Chinese who have lived there for generations, as well as people coming for work from India, the Philippines, Myanmar, and Indonesia.

We visited the Kuala Lumpur Bird Park, which David had been to when he had visited whilst on business some years previously. It was fascinating, particularly because, though covered by massive nets, the birds have a large area where they can fly freely and we could see them at close quarters. The park has also been able to successfully breed some endangered species and release them back into the wild. While we were there, we had the 'ticklish' experience of sitting and dangling our feet in a fish tank. We were feeding the *Garra rufa* fish with the dead skin on our feet. These are small fish who, for some reason, find the excess hard skin on our feet tasty. It seemed a bit odd that we had to pay in order for them to have a free lunch, but it was fun once we got used to the sensation and our feet were much smoother after half an hour's frenzied feeding!

Visiting St George's Church at the time of its 200th anniversary celebrations enabled us to enjoy this National Heritage building. The local authority has helped to finance its recent refurbishment and a road runs past the church called Harmony Street. This is just one example of the efforts that have been made in recent years to build relationships between worshippers from the Christian, Hindu, and Muslim communities.

Through our contacts from Healing Rooms, we met Yu Lin who is an associate director for Healing Rooms in Malaysia. Yu Lin carries the vision and mandate to help open many more Healing Rooms across the nation. We visited three of the four operating in Kuala Lumpur, as well as one in Penang.

Yu Lin is a lawyer, but she also has part ownership of a number of Chinese restaurants in Kuala Lumpur and she took us out to several of them, where we were well looked after.

Up until this point, we had tried to only eat two meals each day, as a strategy to avoid eating too much. However, when we first arrived in Kuala Lumpur, Yu Lin brought us to her home and we had roast chicken and lamb chops with mint sauce – a real treat!

Those who know us well will not be surprised that we found time to visit a couple of jazz clubs. It's amazing how you can forget where you are on these occasions and imagine you are back in the UK, the US, or Australia. One of the things we like about jazz – apart from the music – is that the musicians really appreciate, enjoy, and applaud each other's solos.

We were also privileged to enjoy singing God's music at the Full Gospel Assembly Church on two separate Wednesday evenings and join over 500 people who had come to pray. Many of them were young people, passionate to see God move in the nation. We were humbled and in awe to see so many people meeting together to worship and pray, in the middle of the week. We later heard that during the week when we were in Penang, the prayer meeting had been praying for a lady who had been wrongly imprisoned. As they prayed, God sent down the phenomenon of gold dust on the meeting. We have seen evidence of this before, including gold teeth appearing in people's mouths. When we returned the following week, we could still see the gold dust sparkling on the carpet, and, the lady was released from prison! Why does God do that? Because He can!

Celebration!

And we had a wonderful evening celebrating . . . our 40th wedding anniversary!

Declaration for Malaysia
November

I love you Malaysia. You are so precious to Me. I have longed for you to encounter Me for so long. I have been saddened that those I sent to you with My Good News failed to give the message of how much I love you and My longing to lead you as a nation in My ways; to bring you into a close relationship with Me; to bless you as a nation; to heal the wounds you have inflicted on each other because you did not know that I am your Father.

I have heard My people's cry for the nation; how costly it is for many to commit to Me and follow Me. I will reward your sacrifices; all that you have given up for My sake. I honour your faithfulness to Me. I am pouring out My Spirit on you in these days. I am preparing you to help Me bring in the end-time harvest in your nation. I call you to declare and demonstrate My glory in your families, to your friends and neighbours, in your communities, in your workplace. Do not fear. I will be with you. I will give you courage. I will give you My words. I will use you to declare My goodness as you perform signs and wonders in My Name for My glory.

If you seek first My kingdom, I will bless you; I will guide you; I will provide for you; I will equip you with everything you need to serve Me. I call you to repent of those beliefs and practices which are a corruption of My truth. As I said to My people Israel, I say to you, 'You shall be holy to Me, for I the Lord am holy.' I am calling you to live your lives in purity and truth. This will cause you to be My light in the nation. I call you to release forgiveness to those who have hurt you individually, and corporately as a nation. I call you to ask forgiveness from those whom you have hurt individually, and corporately as a nation. I know the injustice and suffering you have experienced over the centuries, how you have struggled to be born as a nation with its own identity. As you entrust your future to Me, I will guide you and your nation will indeed be one 'whose God is the Lord'.

As you are obedient to Me, I will not only bless your nation, but will use you to bring mighty waves of blessing to the nations.

We flew to Penang and hired a car for the week, which helped us to get around the island. It was easier because, like Singapore, they drive on the left – another relic of the British era.

There was a restaurant called Winter Warmers, where we had proper English tea – delicious! Most of the time we were offered Lipton Yellow Label and not wishing to be offensive to Mr Lipton, it looks a bit like dishwater! We also continued to have unusual breakfasts; we were introduced to banana and cheese roti at a local Indian restaurant. This is a flattened yeasty dough smeared with the chosen flavour and then baked quickly on a griddle. It actually tasted quite nice.

We spent time praying with selected people as well as attending some Healing Rooms training. We also increased our understanding of some of the different issues out there for people who ask for prayer.

One morning, as we were in prayer and preparation, David clearly heard God say that later that day He would heal someone of eczema. Later, we prayed for several people in difficult situations, and finally a lady came in to see us. When we asked our normal question, 'What would you like Jesus to do for you today?' she immediately responded that she wanted Him to punish her manager, her work colleagues and her neighbours for various perceived wrongdoings. She also complained of sleeplessness. Over a period of about thirty minutes, Janet sensitively led her through her pain and anger to a point of peace and forgiveness. David then asked her if she had eczema and she showed him her hands which were covered with the effects of the disease. He told her about the

> word he had received that morning from God and
> about how she was in His appointment book. He
> prayed for her and then Jesus prompted him to anoint
> her with oil, but He wanted her to be drenched in it.
> So, David passed her the little bottle and she washed
> her hands with the oil. She was cured immediately.

The next day at the healing conference, David called her
forward to give her testimony and she showed everybody her
hands. She declared, *'They're like a baby's skin and for the first
time, I slept all night.'* There was tremendous clapping and
cheering, giving praise to Jesus.

On 21 November, we left Penang and flew to Melaka for a
week. Melaka is a significant place spiritually and politically. It
was here that traders first came bringing the Christian message
and it is where the ruins of the oldest church in Malaysia, St
Paul's, have been preserved. St Paul's was built in 1521, and
the gateway to the city, known as 'A Formosa', is nearby. It was
interesting to hear that Melaka, rather than Kuala Lumpur, the
capital, was chosen as the place for the signing of the Treaty of
Independence from British rule in 1990. The local people were
very pleased. Spending a day leisurely exploring the honey-
coloured city centre and visiting the local museum meant we
could enjoy the beautiful St Francis Xavier Church, with its
stained-glass windows and paintings.

In Melaka, we met some amazing people, who looked after
us for the week we spent there. On our first evening, with
only about two hours' notice, eight people appeared and took
us out for supper. The theme of food, photos and fellowship
continued as it had in other parts of Asia. Within a short space
of time, we had been invited to speak at two evening meetings

and lead some training on healing at the weekend. We spent some time preparing for this. They also insisted we had to be called Pastor David and Pastor Janet, as it is their way of honouring those who come to minister.

We really enjoy ministering together and, with God, we make a good team. We had to have an interpreter, as we do not speak any Chinese, except when Janet sang a worship song, 'Follow, follow, I will follow Jesus', she had learned from a Chinese missionary, sixty years previously. She was understood and told she had pronounced it well, so the long-term memory must not be too bad! At the end of our time in Melaka, we were again favoured by God when Junia, one of the people we spent time with, gave us a lift in her car all the way back to Kuala Lumpur.

Once there, Junia facilitated a meeting with another itinerant minister called Pastor Caleb Lim and his wife Belinda. We hope to help connect them with churches in the UK who want to know more about his teaching and experiences with heavenly encounters and open heavens. We also had the privilege of making a hospital visit to a friend of theirs called Karen, who was being treated for lung cancer. We prayed for her – that she would be healed – and for her husband, Chris.

Next, we prepared to leave for Thailand.

CHAPTER SEVEN

Parasols and Baptisms

December

Our arrival in Thailand by air from Kuala Lumpur went smoothly on 2 December. From the moment we touched down at the airport, we were aware we had entered a nation in mourning.

King Bhumibol Adulyadej had died just a couple of months earlier in October 2016, and after seventy years, had been the longest reigning monarch in the world. That makes our Queen the successor to that title. He was revered as a god and there were pictures everywhere of the late king, surrounded by purple and white drapes.

His son Maha Vajiralongkorn had now become king. It would probably be politically incorrect to say anymore! Suffice it to say that on one occasion, we were with several local Christians travelling in a minibus and chatting happily together for about thirty minutes, and then we asked them, 'So, what do you think of the new king?' There was an immediate and stunned silence that lasted for quite a while, before one brave lady replied, 'Well, as foreigners, what do you think?' Clearly, this was just one example of the problems that still exist amongst these polite, but oppressed people.

We flew into Phuket and arrived at the Hotel Baumanburi, which sounds as though it should be in Germany! One nice hotel maid arranged the towels during our visit into swans, fish, and flowers when she cleaned our room. She also arranged Janet's nightdress into exotic shapes and regularly left flower arrangements in the room. We were sorry that she was not on duty the day we left, as we had wanted to show her our appreciation.

To describe Patong Beach, Phuket as 'quite touristy' is probably an understatement. With lots of bars, pubs, clubs, and 'massage parlours', there are tens of thousands of prostitutes on the island. It felt like Las Vegas on steroids. It is so paradoxical, given the censorship of the government, but apparently, they turn a blind eye to this overwhelming vice because of the importance of the tourist trade. It is said that the trade from sex, drugs, and alcohol in the country accounts for around 10 per cent of its national income. There is loud music everywhere 24/7. Thankfully, we were spared this in our hotel, except on 'Elvis Night' when an ageing Elvis lookalike managed to murder a series of Elvis hits for the evening. We escaped as soon as we had finished our meal!

Over the weekend, we explored the area and found the beach. The weather was so hot and humid that after being out for a couple of hours, we needed to retreat to the air-conditioned haven of our room – a repeated necessity for us westerners unused to such high humidity! We enjoyed some incredibly cheap food at one of the street restaurants: no frills, but good value for money.

Once again, we were aware of God's perfect timing and of His immaculate arrangements. We had tried to contact only one person by email, Pastor David Tan, a missionary from Malaysia whose name we had been given while we had been there. Amazingly, he had attended a Healing Rooms training course about ten years previously but had been unable to start a healing ministry in Thailand. We were able to spend quite a long time with him while we were in Phuket and were able to encourage him. As a result, he booked himself onto the very next training course in Australia the following February and immediately wanted to start the first ever Healing Rooms in the country.

On Sunday 3rd, we were collected by Pastor David and taken to his small church. Their building had only recently been acquired through an amazing series of circumstances. We were warmly welcomed by the congregation and later we gave a message, shared some words of knowledge, and prayed for several people. Afterwards there was the inevitable meal, not just tea and biscuits.

We stayed in Phuket until 15 December, enjoying both the local beach, as well as the facilities at the hotel. Janet went on a boat trip, which included snorkelling on some reefs near Coral Island, and met two women from Taiwan. One of the women, who was also called Janet, was a Christian and became excited about the possibility of starting Healing Rooms in Taiwan.

On our last Sunday, we spoke again at Pastor David's church during a service which lasted three hours. The next day, we hired a car and driver for the day and visited some local beauty spots, including waterfalls and an orchid farm where Janet was presented with an orchid stem. After lunch, we visited the highest point on the island. The highlight of the day was visiting the largest jewellery factory in Thailand to select a beautiful ruby ring to celebrate our 40th wedding anniversary. Janet felt much loved. On our return journey, she took the opportunity to talk about Jesus to our lovely lady taxi driver.

We had more reasons to celebrate and praise after David discovered he had left his beloved hat on the bus after we had been into Phuket town. We searched in vain for a suitable replacement and then asked Jesus to provide for us in only the way that He can. You can imagine our delight when we boarded the return bus to find that it was the same vehicle and driver, and that he had found the hat and carefully tucked it away and gave it back to us. God cares about the little things as well as the big things in our lives.

On 15 December, we flew to Chiang Mai, which is about 1,500 kilometres north of Phuket. We had considered going by train, but this would have taken a couple of days – with uncertain sleeping provisions. The Empress Hotel was very grand, quite a contrast to our Phuket hostelry but still cheap by western standards. When we arrived, we experienced a lot of 'favours from the Lord' – unexpected blessings for which we didn't ask or pay. The receptionist told us we had been given a free upgrade, which included a nicer room, one free evening meal, a daily delivery of fruit to our room, a beautiful flower arrangement, and orchid flowers on our pillows every night. We also received many gifts, presents and a red rose each both on our first visit to the restaurant, and again when we had our free evening meal. That meal had about seven courses, with many added flourishes and extravagances. For example, the dessert platter was filled with an elaborately carved pineapple in the shape of a cart filled with all kinds of fruit – a true cornucopia.

In our room they also left a bag full of delicious goodies to eat, which we were able to give to our hosts at Christmas – extraordinary!

We spent several days exploring the city, which extends over a wide area and seems to have Buddhist temples on every corner. After this, we met Mirjam and her husband Pastor Gampon at City Gate Church. They are an amazing couple who have been missionaries in Thailand for twenty-five years. They have seen astonishing provision for their church and now have wonderful premises, which were miraculously funded.

They have planted seven churches in the mountains among the tribal people, who speak different dialects and language.

Just before we arrived, a team of Samoans had come from New Zealand to help with outreach. It was delightful for us to reconnect with people from a nation we had come to love. We were privileged to join them on a two-day trip to an area about 40 miles from the border with Myanmar. The scenery was lush and green, and we accessed the churches along rugged tracks. We needed substantial four-wheel drive vehicles to get the Samoan team up there.

The tribal women in the mountains have a wonderful traditional coloured dress which they wear on special occasions, consisting of beautifully embroidered waistcoats decorated with shiny buttons, leg bands, and headdresses. They reminded us of the pearly queens in London's East End. It was a great privilege to meet with the tribespeople and see their passionate faith. We enjoyed worshipping with them (sometimes in a tune we recognised), hearing their stories and seeing their churches. We prayed with many for healing. One night, we slept in an ethnic hut at a Christian retreat centre and were glad we had a mosquito net to protect us from anything living or dead that might drop through the thatched roof.

Many of the tribal people in the rural north have converted to Christianity. One of the villages had been very poor because the men had been addicted to alcohol and so did not work. This village was transformed because 100 per cent of the men's lives were changed as a result of becoming Christians and starting to work. The government then needed to build an access road as the villagers could then afford to buy motorbikes and four-wheel drive vehicles.

We spent time with Jo and Mark Plummer, who are part of YWAM from the USA and had set up a vision for Business as Mission – something which is close to David's heart. They invited us to a delightful evening to enjoy pre-Christmas mince pies and mulled wine. It was great to connect with others from the west, singing carols around the piano. During the evening, we met a couple from New Zealand called Gordon and Pauline, friends of Julie Calvert, who had become a special friend of ours while we were there.

Ten missionaries from Missions International in Oklahoma, USA invited us to encourage and pray with a number of them for healing. There are over 3,000 missionaries in Chiang Mai, partly because several missionary organisations have transferred their Asian headquarters to Chiang Mai from Hong Kong.

Declaration for Thailand
November

My people of Thailand, I love you. Over the centuries, many have come to share My Good News with you. But your ears have been unable to hear; your eyes unable to see; your hearts have been unable to receive the truth of My love for you as individuals and as a nation. I the Lord am the Creator of all things; I formed you in order for you to have a personal relationship with Me. I live not in inanimate objects such as wood or stone. You do not find what you are looking for – love, purpose, and acceptance – in these things. As a result many are consumed by perversions of love, which do not satisfy, and further entrap you. I have come through My Son Jesus' life, death, and resurrection to live in each person who puts their trust in Me. Worship your Creator, who made all things. You seek enlightenment through your beliefs. I declare over you My Thai people this word from My servant Isaiah:

'The people walking in darkness have seen a great light; on those dwelling in deep darkness a light has dawned' (Isaiah 9:2).

I will make Myself known to you through those who already know Me; I will come to you in dreams and visions, and your eyes, ears and hearts will be made open to Me to receive My truth. You are a spiritual, peace-loving nation; you care about your land; you care about people. I honour these qualities I have given you – ways in which you reflect Me and My love for all that I have made. As you discover Me, you will also discover your destiny, the plans I have for you as a nation, and as individuals. As in other lands, I am calling My church to come together to pray. You often focus on those differences that separate you, instead of all that you hold in common. Remember My prayer to the Father before I went to the cross. I prayed 'that they (believers) may be one, Father, just as You are in Me and I am in You . . . so that the world will believe that You have sent Me.' Don't you realise, My beloved church, that your best witness to the world is when you come together to pray and worship Me. This also releases My power to bring revival to the nations.

On Christmas Eve, we went to an Italian restaurant for an Italian Christmas meal – five different courses of delicious fish dishes. It was a charity meal in aid of a local orphanage, so you can imagine our delight when some of the children arrived and serenaded us all, singing carols and playing local traditional instruments.

It was a privilege to be part of the City Gate community for a brief time. Christmas Day was somewhat different to our normal experience. We joined Pastor Gampon for the service from 9 a.m. to about 11.30 a.m., followed by lunch; not a turkey in sight! Instead, there was traditional Thai food served to about 100 people – curry, rice, salad, noodles, and vegetables. No mince pies or Christmas pudding, but much better for the waistline. Incidentally, we had noticed that David's belt size had dropped a few notches during our time away from home. There was less access to biscuits, chocolates, and cakes. Although Janet did buy him chocolate as part of his Christmas present. Don't worry, there's still plenty of him left!

After lunch, seven people were baptised, having become Christians earlier in the year. That was significant for them, as it clearly marked their decision to leave Buddhism and follow Christ. For some, they could not tell their families, or they would be disowned by them. Unusually, the church had its own baptistry, although we were rather concerned at the sight of the brown water used for the baptisms, particularly when we discovered it had come from the same tap that had been used to wash the vegetables we had been served for our dinner! Each baptismal candidate was presented with a rose.

Later the same day, we were given yet more food when the church organised an enormous open-air barbecue – on Christmas Day!

We had moved from our resplendent hostelry to another hotel called 'Mountain View', although we could not actually see any mountains from there. It was nearer to the town centre and owned by a Christian GP and his wife. It was incredibly cheap. It had treehouses and the most amazing garden, which was more like a tropical rainforest with a jungle of trees, flowing streams, and ponds right in the centre of the city. We really enjoyed our al fresco breakfasts every day.

In order to relax and see the area, we hired a car and a driver for a day and visited Mae Sa, where there is a series of ten spectacular waterfalls that drop down from the mountain over a distance of about 1 kilometre. It was a beautiful climb – although it was tiring! We also visited the Queen Siringit Botanical Gardens, which is formed on the side of a steep gorge, has many exotic species, and an aerial walkway through the trees.

Pastor Gampon also kindly took us on visits to the umbrella and silk factories. The umbrella factory was interesting as you saw the whole production process from beginning to end. As these are traditional parasols they are not waterproof and are probably too delicate to use. We were fascinated to watch as they made the struts and opening mechanism from bamboo wood and the paper covering from mulberry leaves, before preparing and assembling the umbrellas. It was wonderful to see the artistry in the final flourish of hand-painting the creative designs on the finished product. Photos from Princess Diana's visit there in the 1990s were all over the showrooms.

At our visit to the silk factory, we observed the process of making the silk. Janet felt a bit sorry for all the silkworms who gorge on mulberry leaves, make their cocoons, then die when their homes are unravelled around them. It also reminded us of the prophecy from Pastor Roy in Manila, when he had alluded to the significance of the Silk Road from China, and of the 'Back to Jerusalem' movement.

Our final days were spent speaking at the Sunday morning service and at the New Year's celebration and party. Just before leaving, we enjoyed a classic Thai full body massage (our Christmas present to each other) at a beautiful spa located in a well-restored house in the city. Two hours of unknotting muscles ensued – ouch! However, it was worth it in the end. At one point during the facial treatment, Janet had sliced cucumber all over her face, with just a tiny gap for her nostrils. She is glad there was no photo of this, though of course she would have been unrecognisable. They seem to have an abundance of cucumbers in Asia and they generally appear at every meal.

When it came time to leave, our departure seemed to be going smoothly. We checked in early at the airport and were 'chillaxing' – as our friend Roy in the Philippines says – when we heard our names on the loudspeaker calling us to catch our flight, which was just about to take off. We discovered that the airline had mistakenly booked us onto an earlier flight. So we boarded the earlier flight and then when we arrived at Bangkok Airport, where we needed to change flights for Vietnam, we realised why God had rearranged it like that. There were queues everywhere. We had luggage to collect and check in again, and VAT to claim back on Janet's ring. We would never have made it onto our connecting flight if we hadn't arrived early. Another kindness from our heavenly Father. And so, onwards we went on our journey, and . . . 'Good morning, Vietnam!'

CHAPTER EIGHT

Drugs, Motorbikes, and a Wedding

January

On 2 January, we left Chiang Mai and travelled to Vietnam via Bangkok. Only five days before we came to Vietnam, it became clear that Hanoi would be our next destination. We had only one contact, Pastor Chung, whose name had been given to us by a pastor in Melaka, Malaysia, when we had ministered to his Vietnamese expat congregation there.

Pastor Chung met us from the plane in Hanoi and the following day, we met him, his wife and his interpreter, Zung. We had coffee together, and then lunch, by the end of which he had mapped out on the back of a napkin a fourteen-day schedule of ministry at various venues around the city. This included a number of drug rehabilitation centres linked to congregations and various churches and cell groups. These were located in diverse places, such as a sunflower seed processing factory and another making polythene bags.

It was a privilege to share with about twenty-five people who gathered at the sunflower seed factory. After the mandatory rest they insisted we needed, we sat around on the floor and they provided traditional food for us all.

It is important to enable the local congregations in their ministry, and to show that we are nothing special. So we shared about the Holy Spirit and prayed for a young man with back problems who was powerfully healed. When others came forward for prayer, we directed him to pray for a lady with back problems, as we believe that it is important to empower Christians to pray – we have nothing more to offer than they do. We hadn't bargained for what happened next. The lady fell down under the power of the Holy Spirit, so we had to do some impromptu teaching and reassure everyone she was not dead! They had never seen anything like this before.

We were strongly advised that, as we were in a communist country, we needed to be careful about where we shared our faith and to always enter places of worship quickly, as we were westerners, in order to avoid the police targeting the church. There is said to be freedom of religion in Vietnam but there are many restrictions made on those churches who register with the government. Therefore, many churches choose to operate under the radar. Persecution does occur – often in the form of arresting leaders, as well as closing and/or destroying places of worship. Communism has not eradicated faith, and it is notable that Christianity is the only faith that is growing in the nation, although most people still adhere to Buddhism in a nominal way.

Vietnam is a beautiful country. It is very green and fruitful. The people are gentle and respectful, particularly to those who are older. We could not understand why, soon after meeting someone for the first time, they would ask, 'How old are you?' In our own culture this would be unthinkable. We later understood that they have at least six forms of greeting dependent upon our age, and whether we were old enough to be the inquirer's mother or father, grandmother or grandfather, and they were anxious to show proper respect.

Declaration for Vietnam
January

My people of Vietnam, I love you. You have always been in My heart. I have seen your suffering, the blood that has been shed; I have heard the cries of those who do not yet even know My name; I am responding to your longing for hope, love, peace and purpose for your lives. I am giving fresh courage and boldness to my children as they reach out with My Good News.

You will see increase as people with a hunger for the truth discover that I love them; that I am their Healer and Deliverer; I will come to those who are in prison for My sake. I will provide for them supernaturally; it will be as in the days of Elijah when I sent food each day by the ravens. My angels will come and feed you and provide for your needs.

The leaders of your nation will encounter Me, and their lives will be changed. I call on all who love Me to pray for your leaders; to pray for revelation; to bless them and not curse them. As you do this, you will see a turning of the tide in your nation. The controlling spirits that dominate your land will lose their power, and My Spirit of grace, love and forgiveness will sweep through your people.

Many have become disillusioned with a life where there is no meaning, purpose or hope. Even material success that some achieve brings no satisfaction, but instead other problems such as addictions of different kinds. I declare that 'I know the plans I have for you, plans to prosper you and not to harm you, plans to give you a hope and a future' (Jeremiah 29:11). As you continue to seek My face, I am coming to bless and transform Vietnam in these days.

The Vietnamese are hard-working. They are creative, making many beautiful craft items from wood, including intricately carved furniture, as well as complicated designs in woven fabrics and jewellery.

Paddy fields were all around. On our travels, we enjoyed lots of different kinds of rice – sticky, blue, red, black, and white. In the mountainous regions, terraces are carved in the hillsides, in order for rice to be cultivated. They have as many as three harvests a year.

Our days were filled with opportunities to speak, preach, pray for healing, and see people accepting Christ into their lives. We were privileged to meet young men who had been addicted to drugs – some having served prison sentences – who had come to the drug rehab centres run by the church. We visited about six of these centres, which offered very basic facilities – no beds, just a mat and blanket on the floor; simple food, which they prepared, and shared with us when we visited. They told us how they had heard about Jesus' love for them and after prayer and practical care, had come off drugs without withdrawal symptoms. Such is the transformation, that many later become pastors themselves.

We were humbled to meet so many for whom being a Christian is costly, not only risking imprisonment, but having difficulty in securing employment because of their faith. We were impacted by their simple faith, their joy, and the centrality of their relationship with God to their everyday lives. We often taught them about the Holy Spirit and about forgiveness. David spoke about addiction, based upon his own experience, and told them about the two problems they had. There was one little problem and one big problem. The little problem was their addiction and the big problem was the cause of that addiction. They each had a hole in their heart that could only be filled by the love of Jesus. Many of these former criminals were moved to tears.

One weekend, we each decided to engage in different activities. We had been offered the choice of either ministering in Hanoi or joining a team of intercessors who were travelling across the country praying for the nation. We felt that we could do both if Janet joined the team of about twenty for two days, when they travelled north to the mountainous region. David remained in Hanoi visiting various outreaches, teaching and ministering to the sick. He was also asked to give the message at a wedding. He chose to speak about the three-stranded cord, where God needs to be joined to the couple as they unite in marriage.

Janet's trip to the mountains was unforgettable:

I joined a team of Christians who had already been travelling for a week from Ho Chi Minh City in the south, praying for the country, visiting different churches and encouraging them. We travelled from Hanoi north for about six hours, worshipping, praying, and sharing together. When we arrived at the hotel, I was told, 'Now we ride the motorbikes!' This had been mentioned in passing when I had joined the team, but I had conveniently forgotten about it. The prospect of travelling on the back of a motorbike was daunting to say the least. It is not a form of transport I would normally choose. But I soon discovered why motorbikes were being used. After a short distance on a metalled road, we turned onto a rocky mountain track that snaked around, up and down the mountainside. There was no road! Even the bridges looked as if they may not last long. I was scared and probably gave my driver bruises round his middle from holding on too tightly!

On arrival at our destination in the heart of the mountains, about 6 kilometres from the starting point, we found groups of women gathered in the afternoon sunshine, reading their Bibles and sharing together. Dressed in their national costumes of embroidered jackets, colourful skirts and headkerchiefs in honour of our visit, they made an impact on me that I will never forget. Some twenty-five years previously, Vietnamese Christians had arrived in the village expecting to be the first to share their faith with the indigenous people, only to discover that the village had already heard the Christian message on their shortwave radios and had already been converted.

Since then, they have built a splendid church where over 200 people gather each Sunday. The team had brought gifts of linen and clothing with them as the people are extremely poor. I was asked to share some teaching with them, and also ministered to them, including praying for healing, though understanding their needs was a challenge. Everything I said had to be translated, first into Vietnamese and then into Hmong, the local language.

After eating generous helpings of rice, chicken, fish, and vegetables, which were all home produced, we had to mount the motorbikes and return the way we had come. I was assigned a different driver, whose main object was to get back before anyone else (or so it seemed) and he took every opportunity to overtake. We were among the first to arrive back in town. I was relieved to still be in one piece! However, I would not have missed the trip for anything.

Towards the end of our time in Hanoi, we travelled to the coast to Ha Long Bay, another World Heritage site and one of the natural wonders of the world. Neither our driver nor our interpreter from the church had ever visited the area. The following morning, we were up early in order to take a six-hour cruise to see some of the thousands of craggy limestone outcrops and islands scattered across the bay. Again, our hosts had rarely travelled by boat as Hanoi is far from the sea. We sailed gently among the islands, one of which had amazing formations of limestone. With a bit of imagination and creativity, it was possible to see shapes that conformed to mythical creatures and other objects. Amazing caves were lit with extravagant colours for all to enjoy.

It's a Small World

We explored one of the inlets in a bamboo boat, had lunch on board, and in the process met two young guys who were friends, one of whom lives in Brixton – near where we used to live – in South London. The other originally came from Havant – where we now live in Hampshire!

We were pleased that the weather remained fine, although overcast, until we were on our journey back and the rain which had been forecast began to fall. The only excitement on our journey back was being stopped by the police because our driver had supposedly exceeded the speed limit. He meekly paid the fine, whether or not it was justified. It is unwise to challenge the police as they can arrest drivers and impound vehicles with impunity. Often, the fine serves to supplement the police income as no forms are completed. It made us thankful that our own police force in the UK are generally more honest.

Traffic in Hanoi is unbelievable. Although the police are said to enforce the rules of the road in the city of Hanoi, we saw little evidence of this. Red traffic lights appear to be just a suggestion and pedestrian crossings, including those displaying 'green man' symbols, are merely decorations on the road. The one rule seems to be 'Do not stop for any reason'. One evening we needed to cross from our hotel to a nearby restaurant at a particularly busy junction. We stood there for about ten minutes, with absolutely no gap in the unceasing swarm of traffic. Consequently, the only way we could cross the road on foot was to plunge into the hundreds of motorbikes, like swarms of bees buzzing along! Cars and bikes swerved around us until we reached the other side of the road. It was almost as scary as Janet's motorbike experience had been.

While we were in Vietnam, Janet celebrated her birthday. On that day, we had been asked to share with a group of orphans who lived at the church, boys aged around 9 to 15 years. We had felt a little out of our comfort zone as we generally feel more at home teaching adults. However, we were amazed at how unnaturally well-behaved they all were, meekly sitting on the floor around the walls. David realised that they had probably been told to be on their best behaviour. So, speaking about the Holy Spirit, he recounted the events of the first Pentecost. Then he told all the boys to charge around like the rushing wind that had so impacted the apostles in Jerusalem. After that, they really engaged with the things we encouraged them to do, which included praying for each other and drawing prophetic pictures.

As Christians, we often listen to God and ask Him to give us insight about something He wants to show the person we are praying for. Sometimes, this is in the form of written words or drawings. We found that these young people were able to hear God speak to them for their friends in this way. We were learning more about the way God chooses to speak to young people because their spiritual hearing is less cluttered, and their faith is less complicated than for us older ones. We need to actively include young people in the prophetic and healing ministries.

At the end of the session, a birthday cake was produced, iced with Janet's name, and decorated with a roman candle firework. It was just as well there were no smoke alarms! Then they all sang 'Happy Birthday' in Vietnamese and, of course, were delighted to help us eat the cake! What a special treat.

Our departure from Vietnam was initially hampered by a bureaucratic demand that we were required to have a flight booked to leave the Philippines before we could depart Vietnam. We already had a flight booked from Kuala Lumpur to Israel after our visit to the Philippines and would therefore have to leave the Philippines to catch it, but the agent at the flight desk insisted that this was insufficient. However, as a good bureaucrat, he was satisfied when we booked an internal flight to one of the islands in the Philippines, which we knew we were due to visit anyway. We thought they would be glad to get rid of us, especially as our Vietnamese visas were about to expire.

Then, we returned to the Philippines . . .

An Outrageous Couple of Weeks

Back to the Philippines

On 16 January, we were on another plane. For the first time during the whole of our trip (apart from transferring at Kuala Lumpur Airport several times) we were returning to a country we had visited before. Our time in Vietnam had not been without its challenges, so it was delightful to anticipate meeting up with our friends in the Philippines again.

We arrived at Hotel Mabuhay, which in Filipino means, 'welcome', 'to life', 'live great', or 'hello'. We quickly discovered that the hotel was owned by Christians, as they displayed a Bible verse for the day in the main lobby. They also had a room where people could go to pray and worship and there was a form in our room encouraging us to write our prayer requests that would be picked up and used by their prayer team. We later heard from our friends Pastor Roy and Adora that they had been involved in helping to set up the Christian hotel in the first place.

It was located in an interesting area surrounded by a great deal of poverty, with one street so full of homeless people in sleeping bags that we dubbed it 'Street-sleepers alley'. We were saddened to see so many young men for whom life holds little hope. Many are addicted to different substances, which has left them in poverty, and they are often separated and alienated from their families. We are glad that there is hope coming to the Philippines with the help of a device known as SPERA, which means 'hope'.

In contrast to this, only a short taxi ride away there is the very luxurious and totally westernised Mall of Asia, reputedly the largest of its kind in Asia. Here, there is a mandatory bag check, which consists of a cursory poke in your bag by an armed security guard with what looks like a drumstick. After that, it is like being in any shopping mall in Europe or America, plus it has the welcome addition of being air conditioned. This is a great relief when the humidity outside is pretty much 100 per cent and the temperature well over 30ºC! Our evening was spent catching up with our friends Roy and Adora, and BG and Jhoey – over another meal of course.

Two days later, we went back to the flat where Iris Ministries is located in Tondo. While we waited for Jorelli, we were soon surrounded by a group of ten children aged between 4 and 10 years old. It is always amazing how you can find ways of connecting with children when you don't speak their language, even without sweets! We found it really sad to see such young children who have already lost their second teeth to decay, because their diet is so poor. The cheapest available food is McDonald's and Jollibee. Apparently, fresh fruit and vegetables are so expensive that poor families cannot afford them.

We set off for the local hospital, which we had visited when we were there before. This time, we were prepared for the filth and lack of hygiene on the paediatric ward we visited. For example, there were no hand cleansing or washing facilities available for visitors on arrival and the basic procedure of washing hands between attending patients was also missing. These simple rules could prevent a lot of infection and don't cost much money. Our Jewish forebears were able to stay healthier by following these guidelines from the Old Testament. That's the end of that rant, we promise!

We had the opportunity to pray with several sick children there. As before, a number of them were new-borns who had an unsurprising diagnosis of sepsis. We spent some time praying with a little boy called Michael who had been in hospital since before Christmas, after he had fallen and banged his head. He had become unconscious and had not recovered. We were struck by the faith and determination of his stepmother, who believed that God would heal him. We agreed with her and declared life over this frail little 7-year-old. Nothing is impossible with our God.

Later, we were finally able to meet with Dominique (Angel), who heads up Iris Ministries in the Philippines. She shared about a new initiative called *I Dream*. She plans to make a film about the dreams people have, to give them a sense of hope for the future. Dominique was keen to film David's dreams. In fact, just before we left the Philippines we met her again in a coffee shop and she videoed us both sharing our thoughts about dreams and their importance.

While we were there, we had hoped to connect with Heidi Baker as we knew she was visiting at that time, but we missed her by about five days. We had contact with her later and she has been very supportive of what we believe God is calling us to in the future.

Another highlight of our return to the Philippines was a long-planned visit to Tacloban, an island on the east coast. We had a further baggage hassle as we had been unable to increase our luggage allowance online and we were faced with the possibility of an additional fee – three times the normal amount. The only way around the problem was to pay for an upgrade, where your baggage allowance is more generous. For anyone thinking, *it is time those Simmondses sorted out their excess-baggage issues,* please remember that our checked bag and carry-on case (one each) had carried all of our things for a whole year. It may well be true, however, that we need to think about whether there are things in our lives that we would be better without.

Tacloban is famous for a severe storm surge, which hit the island just three years before we arrived. The surge – like a tsunami wave – travelled a considerable distance inland, destroying everything in its path, but with little loss of life. Many of the people who live on the water's edge in shanty housing were made homeless. They make their living mainly from fishing, so although they have been displaced and provided with proper replacement housing much further inland, it is so far from the sea that many have chosen to go back to their makeshift housing in order to be able to continue fishing.

Soon after we arrived, we went with our friends BG and Jhoey, to visit the extremely glamorous Mayor Christina, a former film star, whose husband is a descendant of the Marcos Dynasty. She is a Christian and has done much to improve life for the poor on the island. She has provided many women with sewing machines so that they can produce clothing and other items to supplement the family income. David told the mayor about the SPERA device, which helps people to come off drugs without withdrawal after a week of treatment, along with appropriate follow-up and support. She was excited about this as they have at least 3,000 known addicts in Tacloban. She saw that it could transform the lives of many individuals and families there. We were privileged to be able to pray for her and when we asked her what she needed from God, she said, 'Wisdom, like King Solomon long ago.'

Our weekend there had many facets. We shared in the *Shabbat* meal at the home of the pastors of one of the churches. Although Pastor Milo and his wife Pastor Judy are not Jewish, many Christians in South East Asia honour the Jewish faith by celebrating *Shabbat* and other Jewish festivals. It is through this special people that we have encountered Jesus, who was born into a Jewish family over 2,000 years ago and who has transformed history ever since. It was a great privilege to share this meal, which started with worship. There was also the lighting of the beautiful brass Menorah (a seven-branched candlestick), the reading of traditional Scriptures, and prayer for the parents and children present.

The following day, we went to a Holy Convocation. We didn't really know what to expect as we hadn't attended one before. The gathering consisted of pastors, leaders, gatekeepers (those committed to praying for Tacloban), and apostles. They had expected thirty people but instead ninety arrived. It was an annual meeting, and this was its seventh year.

After worship, BG talked about the way in which he had been used to redesign the paper money and passports for the nation. He later shared about the seven pillars (aka the Seven Mountains), which society needs to have in order to function in the way God planned:

A   Arts

B   Business

C   Church

D   Design

E   Education and Media

F   Finance

G   Government

He encouraged leaders to align themselves to one of these areas and commit themselves to prayerfully use their influence to promote standards, get rid of corruption, introduce godly principles in relationships, and prioritise the needs of the whole community. It was a great privilege for us then to be invited to anoint and pray for the leaders about these areas.

Many of these people were in key positions in the secular world as well as in the church; how we need this in the UK! David had been holding onto God's instruction since meeting

Eddy in Bali and knew that this was the right time to share a message on 'righteousness'. Janet declared what she believed God was saying to the people of Tacloban.

At the end of the meeting, most people came forward for prayer and it was wonderful to see many on their knees praying for God to step in and help them.

Much later in the afternoon, we went out for a late lunch and in the evening, we were enjoying coffee on the hotel rooftop and sharing more about God as Healer. Inevitably, we were asked to pray for those who needed healing and one person was immediately healed of a shoulder injury. Later that evening there was an earthquake, but we didn't feel it, though others in the hotel did; we were quite disappointed!

Sunday worship was held at Pastor Milo's church, and BG shared a challenging message on 'The Threshing Floor', describing the process of the loving discipline that God takes us through as Christians, so that we get rid of the 'chaff' in our lives. It was relevant to the leaders of the church who had to deal with a number of issues locally, which had resulted in some people leaving the congregation. We both shared some prophetic pictures we had been given and later encouraged the whole congregation to surround their pastors and pray for them. Apparently, it was the first time in their fourteen years of ministry in that church that this had happened. It was so encouraging and meaningful for them. After we had been prayed for we were served yet more food.

Next, we went to McCarthy's Landing – the place where the USA arrived when they came to liberate the islands of the Philippines towards the end of the Second World War. It is also the first place that the Christian faith had been brought to the islands. Sadly, it is also the place where Freemasonry was introduced, with the consequent spiritual bondage that still affects many people. We read Psalm 24, blew *shofars*, and read the declaration we had been making over the Philippines since September. BG shared a vision he had received from God when he had been at the beach three years beforehand; about a vast army coming over the horizon from the sea and the ground was shaking. God is moving in the Philippines.

We stayed for two more days and were taken on a tour of the island arranged by Christians in the marketing department at City Hall. It became a prayer tour as we visited places of significance such as the Santo Niño Museum which houses a statue of the baby Christ. It all seemed spiritually dark because many of the local people worship this as an idol and are really superstitious about it. After that, we went to another statue and prayed, making declarations and blowing the *shofar*. It was near the San Juanito Bridge – a beautiful and imposing curving structure which is 2.6 kilometres long.

On our final morning, we arranged for our little grey carry-on case to be couriered to Manila separately as, once again, we had too much baggage for the small plane. We couldn't upgrade or even pay more money; the plane simply wasn't big enough. Little did we know that it would be more than six weeks later and at considerable cost, before we would be reunited. But that is a story for another time!

Our final action was meeting with Mayor Christina again before we left. She wanted to know more about the SPERA device and David was also able to offer her and the Head of Human Resources some input on how the general morale and standards at City Hall could be improved through various management and training standards. He offered his services in training and mentoring to Mayor Christina and others. What a weekend!

After that we set off for Cebu, so that we could meet up with our friend Nicola again and celebrate a significant birthday with her. Eventually, we arrived at Hotel Alta, which our taxi driver had problems finding. Life would be so much less complicated if all taxi drivers had GPS.

We have mentioned before the interesting decor in our surroundings; this particular hotel had a jungle and environmental theme. This was fine, except when we entered our room and encountered an explosion of colour with life-size murals of a leopard, tiger, giraffe, and elephant in lush vegetation, painted all over the walls. It felt like they were watching our every move. We were glad we didn't have small children with us who were prone to nightmares. However, all was well when we switched off the lights.

The next day, Nicola and Janet decided to go snorkelling from an island nearby:

As the trip involved hiring an outrigger boat and crew to take us there, Nicola was a bit nervous as she hadn't done this without a local person to help with communication and avoid being taken advantage of in terms of the cost. However, all went well as it turned out that the owner knew the pastor of the church where Nicola is the youth pastor. Although the costs escalated when it came to having lunch on the island. We have learned that in the Far East (even among Christians), they can inflate the prices or try to make us feel that as wealthy foreigners, we have a duty to give them more money.

Nicola and I thoroughly enjoyed swimming for nearly an hour, looking at the amazing tropical fish. It was sad to see, as in other places, that the coral had been damaged, most likely by environmentally unfriendly fishing methods. They have, however, set aside protected areas where boats are no longer allowed to go, so maybe in another fifty years it will recover. We were aware of the poverty on the island. The community there survive by means of fishing and with income from visitors like ourselves.

Nicola and I had been encouraged to buy snacks from our boat owner to give to the children there and, of course, they crowded around us like bees on a honeypot. Later in the evening, we all went out for a meal at a floating restaurant nearby. It was so picturesque.

We were asked to share with the young people at Nicola's church. They meet every Friday evening to spend time preparing to lead worship on Sunday. Unusually, all seventeen of them came and asked us to teach them about releasing prophetic words for each other. They asked if we could spend time with each of them on their own, listening to what God had to say for them individually. They were a little surprised when what we spoke to each of them reflected what was going on in their hearts.

Another day was spent at a local abandoned beach resort. It was rather disappointing when it started to rain but Nicola's friend and her 4-year-old daughter who came with us, were undaunted. Our visit to Nicola's apartment later that day made us feel very humble. She lives down an unlit, unpaved road, which is not really safe after dark and she constantly battles with keeping the place dry when it rains. She has no hot water for showers. It puts some of our minor inconveniences into perspective. As we arrived at her street, the police were arresting a 17-year-old for a drug offence.

We were reminded again of the importance of offering more tangible support to our missionary friends.

Nicola's birthday was a mixture of work and celebration. We visited the sewing factory which she manages and enjoyed a takeaway Jollibee with the women there and other friends, as well as a lovely birthday cake and flowers for Nicola. We delivered the garments they make to a Fairtrade wholesale outlet called Anthill,[12] which encourages people to maintain their craft skills and sell items they have made, including traditional rugs, carpets, and fabric using tribal designs, and other craft items.

After a memorable celebration meal at a Thai restaurant on the water's edge, we had to say goodbye to our special friend, as we were returning to Manila the next day.

On 29 January, we arrived at Acacia Hotel just in time to meet with our friends BG and Jhoey again, to discover that they worship at the church that meets at the same hotel on Sundays. Afterwards, we went to their home where we met with others to belatedly celebrate both Jhoey and Janet's birthdays. They both share the same birth date on 13 January.

Their house is a wonderful example of design from approximately 100 years ago. It belonged to BG's grandparents and has some significant items of furniture, such as a table used by a former president of the Philippines. We also met Bruce and Elaine Smith, Healing Rooms directors for Adelaide, who have a long-term commitment to the Philippines, particularly in supporting projects for the poor. After an amazing meal, we spent time considering some spiritual strategies to help fulfil God's purposes for these islands.

Roy Carandang later made some stakes from Acacia wood, which we used to put in the ground at various places to symbolise reclaiming areas which have been affected by dark practices such as witchcraft and other occult rituals. We have continued with this, and feel God is calling us to extend the declarations into Turkey. Maybe we will tell you what happens in another book.

---

12. http://www.everythingcebu.com/lifestyle/business/anthill-fabric-gallery/

We survived another early start the next day in order to drive the two hours to Cavite. We were going to visit the ancestral home of Emilio Aquinero who was the first president in the Philippines at the end of the nineteenth century. It is a huge property, standing tall over the surrounding region. It is also significant because the treaty declaring independence from Spain was signed on 12 June 1898 and the new flag was waved there for the first time. Freemasonry was very evident in the house, and was introduced to the islands at this time. The triangle on the flag comes from those roots. We found the house to be quite oppressive, as it had many masonic symbols built into its design – triangles, five-pointed stars, and regalia used in their rituals. As we toured the house, we prayed and anointed the doorposts with oil to cleanse it from occult influences. Later, we climbed to the highest point of the house and read Psalms 24 and 133. We also read the declaration we had been praying over the Philippines. We blew three *shofars* seven times to each of the four points of the compass, as a prophetic act reclaiming the nation for God. We also released three pigeons as a symbol of peace, and Janet sang the chorus, 'Shout to the North', declaring God's lordship over the earth.

Our bemused guide had been watching us praying and talking about God's purposes all morning, and when asked about his relationship with God, he said that he wanted to know Jesus too. We were delighted when he became a Christian there and then. We ended our visit with lunch at a restaurant with Dr Ruth and her husband Joey.

We travelled back to Muntinlupa and hammered our first stake of acacia wood into the ground, quite close to the main prison in the Philippines, where human sacrifices have been made. We reclaimed the ground and sprinkled it with olive oil as a symbol of the Holy Spirit.

Our last evening with our friends Pastor Roy, Adora and their family, was special as we knew we may not see them again for a while.

Two other important events took place on 30 January. We met with Craig, an associate of Dr Graham Giles who was in Manila and who demonstrated the SPERA device to a small group, including a Christian medical doctor. It could be part of the solution to the drug addiction issues affecting thousands of people in the Philippines. This not only affects the addicts and their families financially and emotionally but adds to healthcare costs due to the associated links with tuberculosis and HIV/AIDS from contaminated needles. The detox device will also help addicts to change their lifestyles, as well as contributing to society and helping their families.

At the meeting in a coffee shop in Manila, a senior health practitioner from Tacloban called Dr Gloria asked to wear the device for just half an hour, in order to help her deal with symptoms of stress and sleeplessness. She immediately agreed that this device could help deal with the drugs epidemic, which has increased considerably in the last forty years. There is now real hope that a trial run could take place in the Philippines, given the raised profile to this issue in recent times, particularly since President Duterte came to power, as his particular approach to the solution was rather controversial.

The second exciting event that day was attending a presentation of awards at City Hall in Muntinlupa, organised by 'God Bless Muntinlupa' – a wonderful local Christian organisation that recognises and honours people who have gone beyond the call of duty in their work in local government. What an amazing idea; we should do this in the UK. Our friend BG again shared his vision about the seven pillars. We were then asked to anoint all the award-winners with oil and pray for them, including the Mayor of Muntinlupa and the congressman's wife, Elvie Quiazon. Wow! It could only happen in the Philippines!

Our last day was spent desperately trying to retrieve our luggage that we had left in Tacloban over a week beforehand. To cut a long story short, we were unable to retrieve our luggage after a fruitless taxi ride as we had been given an incorrect address.

Our flight to Kuala Lumpur from Manila went smoothly. We were due to catch a connecting flight to Jordan and then transfer to fly to Tel Aviv. Unfortunately, the check-in desk informed us that our flight had already closed and we would not be able to board the plane. It was now around 11 p.m. and after some investigation, it became clear that there had been a change to the flight which we had booked (several months in advance) and it had been brought forward by two hours. Our travel agent in the UK had been notified by the airline but they had failed to inform us.

We were rather distressed, but in the middle of the night we were eventually able to book another flight (at considerable expense) leaving about two hours later. (N.B. We were finally compensated by the agency for their error some 18 months after the flight!) Our arrival in Israel via Larnaca, Cyprus, was delayed by almost twelve hours. We had not slept in a bed for thirty-six hours. To add to the difficulties, we discovered that our luggage had not been transferred onto the plane at Larnaca. Apparently, this happens quite a lot when an airline decides that the luggage load needs to be reduced, so they leave a whole cart-load behind. We had to go shopping for essentials to survive until our cases arrived. We had arranged a hire car and were looking forward to using our own GPS – who we affectionately named 'Susan' – to find our way to our hotel. Unfortunately we discovered that the maps for Israel had not been downloaded, so we had an interesting time touring the streets of Tel Aviv until we finally found Hotel Gilgal.

Despite all the frustrations and delays, it was a special moment when we finally touched down in Israel. We had a renewed sense of awe about the significance of this land and nation in God's purposes. Although Israel had not been in our original plan, we had come to recognise that this was the right place for us to end our amazing year and this had been confirmed prophetically. So many people on our trip had expressed their delight – and a slight touch of envy – that we would be ending our year-long round-the-world trip in that special land. What would Israel have in store for us?

CHAPTER NINE

The Promised Land

February

After our arrival in Tel Aviv on 2 February, we eventually found Hotel Gilgal, which was located quite close to the sea. It had been recommended to us by friends and is owned by a delightful couple, Jacob Damkani and his wife, who are Messianic Jews. Jacob later gave us a copy of his autobiography, *Why Me?* in which he tells his story of searching for God and how his life changed after meeting his Messiah. The hotel has his amazing mural paintings on the internal walls, as well as some statues outside – one depicting *The Return of the Prodigal Son.*[13]

To our great relief, our delayed luggage appeared the next day – we only had the clothes in which we had arrived. A tour of the city gave us an overview and ended with a trip to the Diamond Exchange. This was a bit of a misnomer as they really want people to buy their diamonds.

We learnt that Tel Aviv means 'hill of spring' and we discovered that 100 years ago it had been a sand dune. David Ben-Gurion, one of the early leaders of Israel, established the first all-Jewish settlement there. Nearby Jaffa (or Joppa) is an old fishing port, which still has many ancient buildings, though little commercial fishing remains.

After a *Shabbat* meal on Friday evening, Jacob shared with us the day's reading from the Torah. On the Sabbath (Saturday)

---

13. https://www.hotelgilgal.com/sysvault/docsgalleries10/cdp6359953625128728577.jpg

we attended a Messianic church, then we enjoyed a walk by the sea in the sunshine. We were pleasantly surprised that it was so warm. Visiting the Diaspora Museum gave us information about the Jewish people's return to the land of their origin from all over the world, where they had been scattered in AD 70, after the rebellion and the rout of Jerusalem by the Roman armies. There was a lot of information about the Ethiopian Jews, who are said to be descended from King Solomon's relationship with the Queen of Sheba. Many have 'made their Aliyah' – returned to Israel following persecution in Ethiopia.

Messianic!

After a few days in Tel Aviv, we travelled to Abu Ghosh – known in the Bible as 'Kiriath Jearim' – a town about seven miles from Jerusalem. Abu Ghosh is said to be the town where the Ark of the Covenant was left in the home of Obed Edom and other households when it was en route back to Jerusalem. Historically, the people of this city welcomed the Jews as they travelled through the land in Old Testament times. Today, the people of the city have repeated history by welcoming Jews when they have returned.

We stayed at the amazing Jerusalem Hills Inn. Our room was called 'City of David' and faced towards Jerusalem. It is owned by the wonderful Chaim and Ruti Singerman and their seven children. They are Messianic Jews originally from Texas, USA. We were most fortunate to meet guests from several different countries, including Kandy, who was volunteering in Israel for a few weeks, helping to prepare accommodation for the Jews who were returning to the land of their forefathers.

In the evening, we went into Jerusalem to enjoy an amazing 'sound and light' show at the Tower of David near the

Jaffa Gate. The show was projected onto the walls of the city and told the history of the people of Jerusalem over the past 3,000 years.

The next day, we decided to visit Yad Vashem, the Jewish Holocaust museum. We had been before but wanted to spend more time there. It was a sobering experience; we were faced with some of the stories of those who died, and some who survived unspeakable suffering and loss. There were piles of shoes, many belonging to children, which graphically illustrated the scale of the horror. It reminded us of man's inhumanity to man and that we all have the potential for such shocking actions, whether it is by ignoring suffering, pretending it isn't there or deciding it isn't our business.

Janet saw an elderly Orthodox Jewish couple walking around the museum and spoke to them, apologising for our nation's failure to do more for the Jewish people during the Holocaust. They were so gracious and thanked her for speaking to them.

Our prayer on visiting Yad Vashem was that this place would not encourage bitterness but instead provoke forgiveness. We have so often seen the releasing healing power of forgiveness. It is as much for the forgiver as the forgiven. We need to learn to honour and respect people from all nations, especially the Jewish people.

On 8 March, we spent more time in Jerusalem visiting the cafe attached to Christ Church, the oldest Protestant church in the Middle East. Built in 1849, after the design of a synagogue, it is called the Jewish church and it celebrates both Christian and Jewish festivals. We had hoped to meet with Canon Andrew White (the 'Vicar of Baghdad') but he was busy speaking to another group of visitors. We did meet him subsequently when he was on his way to 'have cream tea with my friends'. When David introduced himself and said he came from Cowplain (only a hop, skip and a jump from

Andrew's home in England), he exclaimed, '*Cowplain!*' as he embraced David with great excitement.

Later that day, we explored the ramparts of the city, from the Jaffa Gate to the Damascus Gate. There was an unfortunate incident when a group of local teenage boys tried to force us to give them money but being from South London, we just walked through them. We later heard that they had intimidated another group of tourists, who had been forced to turn back. This was our first experience of being threatened during our year away, so we were thankful.

After such an encounter, imagine our joy at being able to walk in Jesus' footsteps in the Garden of Gethsemane.

Following this, we visited the Garden Tomb, which is situated outside the city near the Damascus Gate. We had been there before and it has a much greater authenticity for us than the Church of the Holy Sepulchre.

The Garden Tomb was unearthed in 1867 and many Christians believe that this is the place where Jesus was buried in a rock-hewn tomb, then resurrected three days later. In 1883, General Gordon identified Golgotha, 'the place of the skull', which is described in the Bible as the location of the crucifixion. It happens to be located just above the Garden Tomb, which is in a garden now laid out to make it easier for pilgrims to explore, meditate, pray, and share communion if they wish.

We walked, prayed, and remembered as we shared communion together, with slightly unorthodox symbols of prunes and water! I hope we will be forgiven for that. It meant a lot to us to be able to thank Jesus for the price He paid for us.

We were aware of feeling some oppression during our time in Jerusalem. For approximately ten days we experienced a considerable number of spiritual attacks, including unexpected and unusual problems with:

- Communication and messages
- IT and GPS
- Travel and driving
- Intimidation in the street
- Border guards and security issues
- Cash and credit cards
- Digestion
- Sleep
- Concerns about our own accommodation on our return to the UK
- Relationships
- Theft of David's smart phone

We contacted our good friends in the UK and felt blessed by their faithful support and prayers.

Since receiving our spiritual assignment in the Philippines, we believed that we were due to go to Turkey, where we would visit the Seven Churches of Revelation to pray. We asked some friends to pray for us about these things. Within a short time, we received four email replies offering support and confirming that the visit to Turkey was not right at this time.

Another difficulty we were dealing with was the process of being reunited with the small grey suitcase we had left in the Philippines. It was another example of unbelievable and ridiculous bureaucracy.

On 10 February, we visited the Garden of Gethsemane, where Jesus prayed on the night He was arrested, falsely accused, and found guilty of blasphemy. Some of the olive trees are said to be many hundreds of years old and may have been there at the same time as Jesus.

The church next door has a large stone inside, which is said to be the one Jesus knelt on when He prayed. The Garden of Gethsemane is at the foot of the Mount of Olives, so we decided to walk up the steps to the top. There were 500 steps – Janet counted them! At the top, we were rewarded with a breath-taking view overlooking the city.

Our visit was somewhat spoiled by a young Arab boy harassing us, wanting to 'show us round' or sell us things. He had been standing very close to David and it was only later that we realised that he had stolen David's phone. A visit to the police station to report the incident was a waste of time.

This meant we were without any means of communication with Tom and Kate Hess, who lead the Jerusalem House of Prayer for All Nations at the top of the Mount of Olives. They had invited us to a *Shabbat* meal there that evening. We no longer had their phone number and there was only one place we knew that was near their home, so we headed back to that place. We prayed hard. Fortunately, the hotel owners knew Tom and Kate and we were brought back to their home, known locally as 'The Big House' with a stunning view of Jerusalem.

Tom set up the Jerusalem House of Prayer for All Nations thirty years ago. Since then, Christians have prayed 24/7 in their prayer tower for the nations. Interestingly, the house is owned by a Muslim. Our *Shabbat* meal, with about thirty people present, was preceded by worship led by eight harpists. It was a bit like one would imagine heaven to be.

As their home is situated in Bethany, Tom talked about some of the significant events that took place there. It was the home of Martha, Mary and Lazarus; it was where Jesus raised Lazarus from the dead and where another Mary anointed Jesus with precious oil. It was also Jesus' base during the week leading up to His arrest and crucifixion. It certainly helped us to put the loss of David's phone in perspective.

Tom and Kate were about to leave for Istanbul to lead a gathering of Messianic Jewish leaders from across the Middle East who meet together every year. They wanted to spend some more time with us, so invited us back a few days later.

On the Sabbath, we went to a Messianic Jewish service near Jaffa Gate. Although the songs were in Hebrew, we were able to celebrate God's goodness with them. During our trip, we learnt not to be fazed by different languages and Janet often made valiant attempts to sing the words phonetically. We were reminded by the speaker that we can always rejoice in the Lord because joy is not dependant on what is happening in our lives. It goes deeper than any pain or suffering in our lives. We had the opportunity to pray with some of the people at church, both before and after the service.

We had the delight of meeting Pieter and Monika at the beginning of the service. Monika used to lead the Lydia Fellowship in Austria. This is a worldwide network of women who meet in small groups to pray for their nations. They had both made their Aliyah and moved to Israel to serve God there. We enjoyed a delightful meal in an Armenian restaurant, where the food was basically Middle Eastern.

Later they took us down many little alleys in the city to see the 'non-tourist' parts. We prayed at the Wailing Wall, the only part of what used to be the Temple, now available for Jews to come and pray. We also went to the Little Wailing Wall, found deep in the Arab quarter. Here, Jewish men and women are not segregated and can come to pray side by side.

We observed Orthodox Jews who wear different styles of hats according to whether they are Sephardic, Ashkenazic, or nominal in belief and practice. We learned from meeting with them that they prefer to be called Jewish people; possibly a reflection of their experiences of anti-Semitism. Jewish people who are believers in Yeshua often describe themselves as Complete or Messianic Jews, having encountered Jesus, the Messiah or Mashiach. In past centuries, there has been a demand that Jews must convert to Christianity, but the truth is that they have now met with their long-awaited Messiah and become 'complete Jews'.

As Gentiles, we are the ones who have needed to be converted or 'grafted in' as Paul describes it. So much prejudice is the result of ignorance. Orthodox Jewish people are sometimes warned never to read or even touch the New Testament and so they live in ignorance of the amazing way that Jesus fulfilled all the prophecies made about the Messiah in the Old Testament. Likewise, some people are unaware that Jesus was born into a Jewish family of the lineage of King David and fail to recognise that the nation of Israel is significant in God's plans.

We were able to replace David's mobile phone a few days after it was stolen which meant we could catch up with emails and make Skype calls to family. We also went to a place called Rishion Lezion, a town about 40 miles west of Jerusalem, where we met Pastor Michael Yaron and his wife and family. Michael is Jewish, a medical doctor, and now pastors a church alongside providing a ministry of offering care, respite, and prayer for those who need a break.

Michael and his wife deliberately bought a large home so that they could accommodate visitors. They showed us the splendid bedroom with en suite, which they offered to us if we came back there. As with so many leaders, they give out so much to others, and it was an honour to be able to pray with them about renewing their vision and strength.

On Monday 13th, we went to Bethlehem. Originally, we thought we would drive in our hire car but we were advised that there could be difficulties as we would be visiting the West Bank. Instead, we booked a taxi with an Arab driver who had the 'correct' number plates. We had a smooth trip, both in and out of the city. We had visited all the tourist sites ten years before but wanted to return to a Palestinian Christian cooperative[14] that sells beautiful hand-carved olive wood items and other souvenirs. They have great difficulty in selling their goods because of the restrictions placed on them by the wall erected between Israel and the West Bank some years ago, so it was good to buy quite a lot from them for ourselves and for Manna Christian Centre in London.

Later, we met again with Kate Hess at 'The Big House' and spent two hours in the prayer tower, worshipping and praying for the nations. We felt really affirmed as Kate described us as Abraham and Sarah – well we certainly had been on an epic journey! We felt encouraged and hoped to retain contact with them.

Before we left Jerusalem, we had a call from David Parks, asking if we could come to the Korean House of Prayer in the city. We were a little uncertain about this, as there had been difficulties in setting up the visit, with some miscommunication. We agreed to go, found the place easily, then spent three hours ministering to most of the people there. Ken, who is a prophet and leader from Paul Yonggi Cho's church in South Korea, asked us to pray as he had a diagnosis of rectal cancer. We led him in prayers of forgiveness to those who had hurt him in the past and he described, 'feeling the angels putting a new rectum in'.

Others needed prayer for problems with haemophilia, thyroid, gallbladder, and barrenness. We also prayed for Helen who, for the previous eighteen years, had a large football-sized tumour growing from her jaw. We saw hope come into her eyes as she believed the Lord was touching her. We encouraged her to continue to pray in faith and asked her to send the photo when the tumour disappears.

---

14. http://www.hlhcs.org/

Galilee

We arrived at King Solomon Hotel in Tiberias and discovered that our room overlooked the Sea of Galilee – so beautiful! When we arrived in our room, there was a beautiful bouquet of red roses which were from David as it was Valentine's Day. Janet felt so loved.

Beyond the Sea of Galilee – or Lake Gennesaret as it is also known – we could see the Golan Heights and Jordan. Throughout our stay, the lake remained as calm as a millpond, although we know from biblical accounts that the lake is renowned for its sudden storms.

On 15 February, we met with Kandy (from Jerusalem Hills Inn) at the Aliyah Return Centre. This is a *kibbutz* recently taken over by Messianic Jews, which needed a lot of refurbishment after being abandoned for a number of years. It is a 40-acre site, located on the River Jordan, though it was overgrown with weeds. They had only been there for three months but had made amazing progress with volunteers from the USA, UK, South Korea, and Canada all giving their time and skills.

We met Dean, who heads up the project and has found great favour with government agencies. David shared a word about 'Promise, Possession and Presence' – the land was promised but needed to be possessed in order that God's presence would come.

Later, we went into Tiberias for a meal at an Israeli restaurant – delicious! The next morning, we discovered a rather soggy parking ticket that we had acquired the night before, not realising we had to pay for parking at 8 p.m. However, the hotel manager dealt with it by having a chat with his 'cousin' and we did not have to pay the fine.

Our visit to Capernaum was like a journey back in time. Peter, his whole family and his mother-in-law lived in a house there. We were greatly impacted; it was easy to imagine Jesus worshipping and preaching there 2,000 years ago.

Nearby, was an amazing relic discovered over thirty years ago by a local villager. It is called the Ancient Galilee Boat and was discovered in the mud when the waters receded because of a drought. It took a long time to extract, then it was soaked in preservative for ten years – similar to the Mary Rose in Portsmouth. It is about 2,000 years old and would have been used when Jesus was there.

Declaration for Israel
February

My much beloved children of Israel. Long ago I chose you from all the nations of the earth to share My truth, My heart. You have faithfully carried My revelation down the millennia; you have preserved My words, My teaching and the faith delivered to you. You have suffered much down many generations; sometimes I have disciplined you because of your disobedience; others inspired by My enemy, Satan, have sought to eradicate you from the earth because he has some understanding of your significance as a nation, and your continued role in My eternal plan and purpose of redemption for the whole earth.

But I have always preserved a remnant who has remained faithful to Me. Israel, you are My first born. Your restoration as a nation to the land I gave you long ago demonstrates My love for you. You have carried My truth and passed it on to succeeding generations, with the promise that one day your Messiah would come. I kept that promise 2,000 years ago, when I sent Yeshua, My beloved Son to a humble family, fulfilling all the prophecies I gave you about His coming, birth, life, death, and resurrection, and return to heaven, and now soon, His return at the end of this dispensation. In these millenia, I have revealed Myself to the Gentiles, and many have embraced My Son, Yeshua. I always planned salvation for the ends of the earth, the whole world, and at the end of time, I will parade you with all those other nations who honour Me and My Son.

Many in the nation have recognised, accepted Yeshua, and in these days, I am moving by My Spirit to restore you to Myself as a nation. I am bringing fresh revelation to My people, showing them what has been hidden for so long. Let me remind you, My chosen ones, that 'I cannot forget you. Your name is engraved on the palms of My Hands' (Isaiah 49:16).

I honour you, My people, and like the prodigal son, I welcome you home. I have so much to show you. All the richness of the heritage you value is also precious to Me. My new covenant through Yeshua, fulfils all that you have treasured and looked for. You will discover that I am your loving Father, who has longed to embrace you, to show you that I want to have a close relationship with you, made possible through My Son.

'I am doing a new thing' in your nation. Open your eyes to see that you are My chosen ones, 'the people I formed for Myself that they may proclaim My praise' (Isaiah 43:19, 21) I will continue to bless you and preserve you as I promised long ago.

On 17 February 2017, we went to Nazareth. David had visited the Nazareth Village[15] when we had visited Israel before. This is a living museum, with people dressed as they would have been 2,000 ago. They also show various crafts, like woodcarving, carpentry, spinning, weaving, and shepherding. They grow olives, crush them, and produce olive oil. We were shown the olive press, which was also the name given to the Garden of Gethsemane where Jesus prayed. The first pressing of the olives produces the best oil, traditionally used in the Temple. The second pressing is good for cosmetics and cooking. The third pressing would be used to fill the oil lamps. We were reminded how the Lord was crushed three times as He prayed at the site of the olive press in the Garden of Gethsemane.

---

15. http://www.nazarethvillage.com/

The Nazareth Village is run by Arab Christians, who discovered an old wine press and terracing used to grow grape vines when they excavated the site. It was a fascinating insight into life in Nazareth in the days of Jesus.

On *Shabbat*, we attended a Messianic fellowship in Tiberias. Soon after we arrived, a group from the Aliyah Return Centre, including Kandy, arrived. We enjoyed the multicultural worship and had the message translated for us via headphones. Afterwards, we went out with our new friends to a lovely restaurant overlooking Galilee.

The following day we travelled with Kandy back to Nazareth and attended an Arab Christian Fellowship. We had a car full as two other friends came as well. The fellowship was started by the pastor fifteen years previously but it was only in the last four years he and his family had 'made their Aliyah' to Israel from the USA.

Apparently, the living museum we had visited was set up and run by some of his church members. While we were there we saw a young family, who had converted from Islam just one year before. Now they brought their family to church and it was wonderful to see their joy and excitement as they worshipped together. We also enjoyed watching the young children playing outside and reaching out for their fathers and crying, '*Abba!*'

Afterwards, we enjoyed lunch out with the pastor, who later invited us all back to his house for coffee. We learned that many Ethiopian Jews, who have not been so readily accepted by their fellow Jewish people, have settled in this area. We were saddened to see racism in so many parts of the world.

On 20 February, we travelled north to the Hula Valley Nature Reserve in the north of Israel. We journeyed through a varied landscape, with mountains and even some vineyards. We saw the snow-capped Mount Hermon on the borders of

Lebanon and Syria. This reserve was the first of its kind in Israel and since it was established in 1964, it has become a resting place for many migratory birds from Europe to Africa, giving bird-lovers an opportunity to see thousands of birds en route to and from Africa.

During our visit we watched a 4D interactive presentation about bird migration. This included having our seats tipped back, being nose-dived by planes and birds, splashed with water and feeling animals scurrying around our legs as we followed the flight path of the birds. We shared the experience with a class of schoolgirls, who screamed throughout the performance! As a result, we're not sure how much information we retained afterwards. The whole thing was memorable anyway.

On our way back to Jerusalem Hills Guest House where we were staying overnight, we visited the Sukkot Hillel House of Prayer. We then went to New Gate to make a prophetic declaration, which involved repenting of Britain's failure to honour the Balfour Declaration in 1917. The British Foreign Secretary, Lord Balfour favoured, 'the establishment in Palestine of a national home for the Jewish people.' The land identified was subsequently reduced by 77 per cent in order to appease the Arabs. We could also have done so much more to help Jews who tried to escape in the Second World War.

We read Psalm 24, put one of the acacia wood stakes we had brought from the Philippines into the ground, as a symbol of staking God's claim on this land and the connection between New Gate, Jerusalem and the UK. We shared communion and poured both oil and wine on the stake. We had thought there might be some opposition to what we were doing as we were in the Arab quarter. We ended by blowing the *shofar* three times. Our last task was to retrieve our long-delayed carry-on case from FedEx, although we nearly forgot to do that!

Our journey to Eilat took about five hours and soon after leaving the north, we travelled through desert for 200 miles. David was rather nervous when he realised that there were no petrol stations! When we arrived at Club Hotel, we could see it was rather different from our previous accommodation! It was big and noisy, with a number of swimming pools, though it was too cold to use them when we arrived. We slept in our 85th bed since leaving the UK. During our last few days we rested and enjoyed some sun. Janet went snorkelling in the Red Sea and was able to see a better range of corals than on previous expeditions. Meanwhile, David had a relaxing massage.

Our visit to Timna Valley was a highlight of our trip south. This was an amazing area, just a few miles north of Eilat in the Negev desert. It has striking rock formations developed over the millennia. In the park, there is an oasis and a full-size replica of the Tabernacle, following the detailed instructions given in the Bible in terms of the overall size, construction, and layout. The only materials they have not used are gold, silver, bronze and precious stones.[16]

After they left Egypt and were journeying towards the land God had promised them, the children of Israel were told by God to build the Tabernacle. This would be the place where He came to speak to the people through Moses, as well as the place where they would make sacrifices of various animals as part of their worship. Being able to see it and having explanations about what happened there, as well as the symbolism of the different materials used, was helpful. Our Christian guide explained the parallels with the sacrifice Jesus made for our sins when He died on the cross.

Since AD 70, when Jerusalem was destroyed (including the Temple) there have been no more animal sacrifices offered

---

16. https://www.youtube.com/watch?v=M23-xmCJpUI

there. As Christians, we know that since Jesus has died for our sins and risen from the dead, we no longer need to make any offerings for our sins. We have been completely forgiven.

That evening, we attended another *Shabbat* meal in Eilat with Messianic Jews who run cheap hostel accommodation at The Shelter for travellers as a means of providing for them and reaching out with the gospel. On *Shabbat*, we returned to The Shelter and enjoyed worship there. We met people from Russia, Poland, the USA, and the UK. The message was translated into various languages including English.

During our last two days in Israel, we visited a botanical garden on the outskirts of the city. Until seventeen years before that, it was a guard post as it is near the border with Jordan. It is now an oasis of trees, shrubs, and plants from many countries with a similar climate. They have made an artificial rainforest, which has 'showers' every thirty minutes. An archaeologist had given them a 1,200-year-old fig tree seed which was found at a dig. It was still thriving after four years.

Then, we had a long drive back through the desert of Zin to Tel Aviv. This time, we made sure we had plenty of fuel! Next, it was on to the last plane journey of our epic trip.

Our trip has greatly impacted us and changed us in many ways, hopefully for the better! We wonder what God has in store for us next!

Conclusion

At the time of writing, a few years after our return, we have reflected on our gap-year adventure with God. What has He taught us?

Through our year with Him, Jesus has taught us that:

- ✓ He is in complete control
- ✓ We don't need to be anxious about anything
- ✓ His timing is perfect
- ✓ His miracles are awesome

He has taught us to:

- ✓ Expect the unexpected
- ✓ Trust in Him
- ✓ Delight in His amazing creation
- ✓ Enjoy His wonderful people

Above all, He has taught us to be:

- ✓ Humble
- ✓ Faithful
- ✓ Obedient
- ✓ Adaptable

We hope you have enjoyed our journey too.

Please stay in touch.

David & Janet

dsimlewin@aol.com